THE FACES OF JESUS

THE FACE

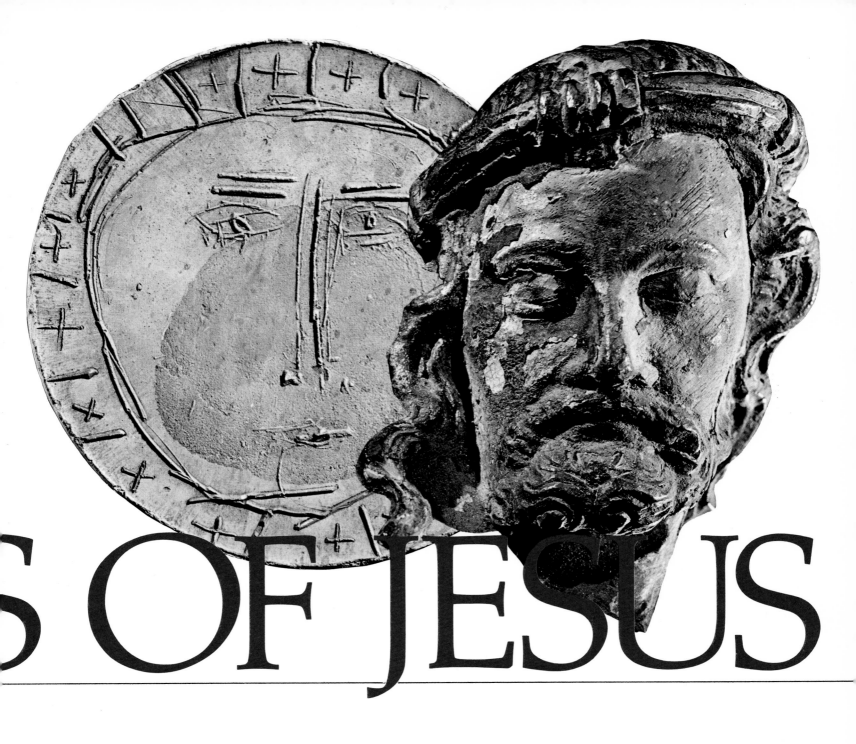

S OF JESUS

Text: Frederick Buechner

Photography: Lee Boltin

Design: Ray Ripper

A Riverwood/Simon and Schuster Book

Published in the United States of America by

Riverwood Publishers Limited, Croton-on-Hudson, New York

and Simon and Schuster, New York.

ISBN: 671-21895-6

Library of Congress Catalogue Card Number: 74-12611

Excerpts from the text and portions of the
illustrations appeared in the November, 1974
Smithsonian Magazine. *1974 by Riverwood*
Publishers Limited.

Conceived by

GERALD STEARN

Project Staff

Art History: Constance Lowenthal
Religion: Gaynell Bordes Cronin
Editorial: Dorothy M. Stearn
Picture Editor: Ray Ripper

This book was typeset in Palatino by Typographic Art
Incorporated of Hamden, Connecticut

Printed and bound in Italy by Mondadori Editore

CONTENTS

INTRODUCTION

He had a face...

Whoever he was or was not, whoever he thought he was, whoever he has become in the memories of men since and will go on becoming for as long as men remember him — exalted, sentimentalized, debunked, made and remade to the measure of each generation's desire, dread, indifference — he was a man once, whatever else he may have been. And he had a man's face, a human face. So suppose, as the old game goes, that we could return in time and see it for ourselves, see the face of Jesus as it actually was two thousand years of faces back. *Ecce homo*, Pilate said — *Behold the man* — yet whatever our religion or lack of it, we tend to shrink from beholding him and play our game instead with Shakespeare's face or Helen of Troy's because with them the chances are we could survive almost anything — Shakespeare's simper, say, or a cast in Helen's eye. But with Jesus the risk is too great; the risk that his face would be too much for us if not enough, either a face like any other face to see, pass by, forget, or a face so unlike any other that we would have no choice but to remember it always and follow or flee it to the end of our days and beyond. Like you and me he had a face his life gave shape to and that shaped his life and others' lives, and with part of ourselves I think we might turn away from the mystery of that face, that life, as much of the time we turn away from the mystery of life itself. With part of ourselves I think we might avoid meeting his real eyes, if such a meeting were possible, the way that at certain moments we avoid meeting our own real eyes in mirrors because for better or worse they threaten to tell us more than we want to know.

With part of ourselves. But there is another part, the

3. Virgin and Child. *Ivory. Byzantine, Constantinople, 11th century.*

9

dreaming part, the part that runs to meet in dreams truths that in the world itself we run from. Thus it is tempting to say that this is a dream book, a book not about the face of Jesus as it really was but about the face of Jesus only as for twenty centuries men have dreamed it was. Yet in the last analysis, this is a distinction that is hard to hold. When it comes to the real truth of a face, the truth that finally matters, who is to say that a dream does less justice than a camera can?

To say he had a face is to say that like the rest of us he had many faces as the writers of the Old Testament knew who used the Hebrew word almost exclusively in its plural form. To their way of thinking, the face of man is not a front for him to live his life behind but a frontier, the outermost, visible edge of his life itself in all its richness and multiplicity, and hence they spoke not of the face of a man or of God but of his faces. The *faces* of Jesus then — all the ways he had of being and of being seen.

The writers of the New Testament give no description of any of them because it was his life alive inside them that was the news they hawked rather than the color of his eyes. Perhaps, when you think the world is on fire, you don't take time out to do a thumbnail sketch. Nobody tells us what he looked like, yet of course the New Testament itself is what he looked like, and we read his face there in the faces of all the ones he touched or failed to: in Peter's face as he sat at dawn by the high priest's fire and heard the cock crow all the ghosts back to their rest except his own, or in the face of Judas leaning forward to plant his kiss in the moonlit garden; in the face of the leper, the wise man, the centurion, Mary's face. You glimpse the mark of his face in the faces of everyone who ever looked toward him

4. Crucifixion. *Serigraph. Sadao Watanabe. Japan, 1970.*

or away from him, which means finally of course that you glimpse the mark of him also in your face too.

Then you turn toward his face itself the way you might turn from shadows on the wall toward the light that cast them or from the storm lashing at your porthole you might sail on into the eye of the storm where everything is still. The face of Jesus as light and stillness.

He set his face to go to Jerusalem the Gospels say, sets it like a table or a clock for a time which he does not have to be a God to know is coming as he latches his feet under

11

the soft belly of the ass he rides.

He rises from the table to stand there in silence, and if, like a rose, time itself has a center, a heart, his face is that center, as faith beholds it, and all our times pulse out from it like petals as he raises his life to his lips, his death.

At the end, he is dimly appalled at how little he is given to know. Knows that the tongue he used to talk with is dry and thick as a stone. Knows that there are faces he once knew watching him, that there was a holy man in a river once, a woman somewhere who drew water from a well. Knows that there is a wine-soaked rag held up to him like a woman in labor as he knows he also must labor now to thrust and anguish out into the howling world himself.

His head has slipped sideways like luggage, but the crazy crown remains in place. Like Buddha under the Bo tree, he, on his tree, has his eyes closed too. The difference is this. The pain and sadness of the world that Buddha's eyes close out is the pain and sadness of the world that the eyes of Jesus close in. He is black, cut out of wood by a man with a black face. Paul writes: *God, who commanded*

5. Christ Crowned with Thorns. *Wood.*
Philippines, 20th century.

the light to shine out of darkness, hath shined in our hearts to give the light of the knowledge of the glory of God in the face of Jesus Christ, and to at least one part of that even unbelief can say amen: that it would take no less than God, if there were a God, to enable men to see God's glory in that shambles of a face.

Paul saw it, and for centuries all sorts and kinds of men have seen it — bright ones and stupid ones, good ones and bad ones, young ones and old ones — until little by little they come to look like what they dream toward. Paul saw that too, saw faith as transfiguration, as the faltering growth toward glory of even fools and rascals like himself.

13

This was the final mystery as he understood it, and at the farthest reach of his understanding he tried to set it down as such in black and white. What is the ultimate purpose of God in his creation? To make worlds, to make men, to make life in all its wildness and beauty? *The whole creation groaneth and travaileth in pain together until now*, he says — for all we know, God himself groaneth and travaileth — until the last grim hold out finally capitulates, is transformed *unto a perfect man, unto the measure of the stature of the fullness of Christ*. In other words, the ultimate purpose of God in his creation is to make Christs of us, Paul says.

So once again, for the last time or the first time, we face that face — all the ways men have dreamed it down the years, painted and sculpted it, scratched it into the teeth of whales, stitched it into wool and silk, hammered it out of gold. There it is. Here on these pages it is as we leaf our way through them for one reason or another or for maybe no reason at all. Take it or leave it, if nothing else it is at least a face we would know anywhere — a face that belongs to us somehow, our age, our culture; a face we somehow belong to. Like the faces of the people we love, it has become so familiar that unless we take pains we hardly see it at all. Take pains. See it for what it is and, to see it whole, see it too for what it is just possible that it will become: the face of Jesus as the face of our own secret and innermost destiny:

The face of Jesus as our face. □

``He had

a

face.''

6. Christ Carrying the Cross. *Fresco. Giovanni Canavesio. France, La Brigue, about 1492.*

FOLLOWING PAGE

7. Christ the Judge. *Marble. Nicola Pisano. Italian, about 1270.*

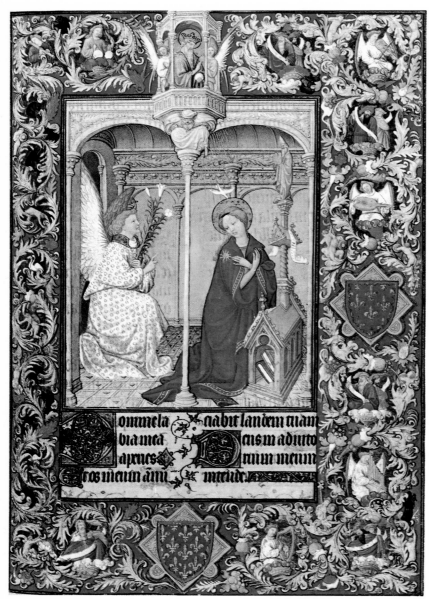

ANNUNCIATION

"Before Abraham was," Jesus said, "I am." Who can say what he meant? Perhaps that just as his death was not the end of him, so his birth was not the beginning of him.

Whatever it is that history has come to see in him over the centuries, seen or unseen it was there from the start of history, he seems to be saying, and even before the start. Before Abraham was—before any king rose up in Israel or any prophet to bedevil him, before any patriarch or priest, Temple or Torah—something of Jesus existed no less truly for having no name yet or face, something holy and hidden, something implicit as sound is implicit in silence, as the Fall of Rome is implicit in the first atom sent spinning through space at the creation. And more than that.

Jesus does not say that before Abraham was, he was, —but before Abraham was, he *is*. No past, no future, but— only the present, because only the present is real. Named or unnamed, known or unknown, there neither has been nor ever will be a real time without him. If he is the Savior of the world as his followers believe, there never has been nor ever will be a world without salvation.

But even for the timeless, to enter time is to divide it into before and after, then and now, just as to enter space is to divide it into here and there, me and you. What-ever the story of Jesus may be to the high angels, to us it must like any other story involve a beginning. The place where his story begins is someplace. The time when it be-gins is sometime. The person it begins with is a girl:

"And in the sixth month the angel Gabriel was sent from God unto a city of Galilee, named Nazareth, to a virgin espoused to a man whose name was Joseph, of the house of David; and the virgin's name was Mary.

"And the angel came in unto her, and said, 'Hail, thou that art highly favored, the Lord is with thee: blessed art thou among women.' And when she saw him, she was troubled at his saying, and cast in her mind what manner of salutation this should be.

"And the angel said unto her, 'Fear not, Mary: for thou hast found favor with God. And, behold, thou shalt con-ceive in thy womb, and bring forth a son, and shalt call his name JESUS. He shall be great, and shall be called the Son of the Highest: and the Lord God shall give unto him the throne of his father David: and he shall reign over the house of Jacob forever; and of his kingdom there shall be no end.'

"Then said Mary unto the angel, 'How shall this be, seeing I know not a man?'

"And the angel answered and said unto her, 'The Holy Ghost shall come upon thee, and the power of the Highest shall overshadow thee: therefore also that holy thing which shall be born of thee shall be called the Son of God. And, behold, thy cousin Elisabeth, she hath also conceived a son in her old age: and this is the sixth month with her, who was called barren. For with God nothing shall be
impossible.'

10. The Annunciation. *Fresco. Ambrogio and Pietro Lorenzetti. Italian, second quarter of the 14th century.*

"And Mary said, 'Behold the handmaid of the Lord; be it unto me according to thy word.' And the angel departed from her."

You cannot see her very well (10). The paint has faded, flaked off in places. She seems to have risen in a hurry and fled to the far side of the room near a slender column. The wall behind her has been mostly rubbed away by the years and the tiled floor too so that there is no solid ground beneath her feet. Her hands are crossed at her throat and her head is bowed, her eyes closed.

11. The Annunciation. *Fresco. Spinello Aretino. Italian, late 14th century.*

She has closed her eyes because what is most unreal in that room is suddenly what is most real: an angel who kneels there facing her with his rainbow-colored wings spread wide and holding in his left hand a branch of olive, that symbol of peace between God and man which the dove brought Noah on his ark so that he would know that the anger of God was past and the waters of the flood rolled back.

The angel says, "Don't be afraid, Mary." He tells her not to be afraid because the floor has failed her and the sheltering wall no longer gives her shelter; not to be afraid because most of what is familiar to her has faded and flaked away including her own flesh. Heaven has flooded in through the ruined wall and welled up where the tiles once were, and Heaven kneels before her now with outstretched wings, but she is not to be afraid.

She is not to be afraid of all that lies beyond her wall-less room — a lonely birth on a winter's night, a child she was never to understand and who never had time to give her much understanding, the death she was to witness more lonely and more terrible than the birth. *"Behold,"* the angel says, "you will conceive in your womb and bear a son." Behold. He is telling her to open her eyes.

The Annunciation. As the ancient prophecies foretold, it is a virgin who is to bear the holy child. "The Holy Ghost shall come upon thee," the angel announces, "and the power of the Highest shall overshadow thee." It is not old Joseph but God who is the father. Paul, Mark, Matthew, the earliest writers about Jesus, say nothing of a virgin birth, but by the time Luke wrote his gospel, it had come to seem that nothing less wonderful could account for the wonders he was gospeling. This extraordinary life could have had a beginning no less extraordinary. History creates heroes. Heredity is responsible for human greatness. Evil also evolves. Only holiness happens.

Mary pondered these things in her heart, and countless generations have pondered them with her. She is sitting on a gothic throne (11) with her hands crossed at her breast and the book she has been reading open on her lap. The dove of the Holy Ghost hovers in the archway above her, and Gabriel kneels close by with a lily in his hand this 27 time, the emblem of purity, chastity, kingship.

12. The Annunciation. *Wooden core, silver gilt, copper gilt, enamel and filigree. Nicolas of Verdun. Mosan, 1205.*

Again Mary's head is bowed, and she looks up at him through her lashes. There is possibly the faintest trace of a skeptic's smile on her lips. "How shall this be, seeing that I know not a man?" she asks, and the angel's painted gaze turns her question back upon herself. The angel, the whole creation, even God himself, all hold their breath as they wait upon the answer of a girl.

"Be it unto me according to thy word," she finally says, and jewels blossom like morning-glories on the arch above

them. Everything has turned to gold (12). A golden girl.

``History creates heroes... Only holiness happens.''

A golden angel. They are on their feet now. Their knees are bent to a glittering rhythm. Gabriel's robe swings free about his ankles, and his scroll flies out from his waist like a sash. Mary's hands are raised, palms forward, and Gabriel reaches out to take one of them. They are caught up together in a stately, golden dance. Their faces are grave. From a golden cloud between them and above, the Leader of the Dance looks on.

The announcement has been made and heard. The world is with child. ☐

13. The Virgin of the Annunciation. *Stone, with traces of polychrome. French, 14th century.*

FOLLOWING PAGES

14. Annunciation. *Brayer drawing; ink on paperboard. Ann Raymo. American, contemporary.*

15. The Annunciation. *Oil on panel. Petrus Christus. Flemish, about 1444.*

16. The Annunciation. *Oil on panel, center of a triptych. Robert Campin. Flemish, about 1425.*

NATIVITY

Some say that ever 'gainst that season comes
Wherein our Saviour's birth is celebrated,
The bird of dawning singeth all night long;
And then, they say, no spirit dare stir abroad,
The nights are wholesome, then no planets strike,
No fairy takes, nor witch hath power to charm,
So hallowed and so gracious is the time.

So hallowed and so gracious is the time—these lines from the first scene of *Hamlet* in a sense say it all. We tend to think of time as progression, as moment following moment, day following day, in relentless flow, the kind of time a clock or calendar can measure. But we experience time also as depth, as having quality as well as quantity—a good time, a dangerous time, an auspicious time, a time we mark not by its duration but by its content.

On the dark battlements of Elsinore, Marcellus speaks to his companions of the time of Jesus's birth. It is a *hallowed* time he says, a holy time, a time in which life grows still like the surface of a river so that we can look down into it and see glimmering there in its depths something timeless, precious, other. And a *gracious* time, Marcellus says—a time that we cannot bring about as we can bring about a happy time or a sad time but a time that comes upon us as grace, as a free and unbidden gift. Marcellus explains that Christmas is a time of such holiness, that the cock crows the whole night through as though it is perpetually dawn, and thus for once, even the powers of darkness are powerless.

Horatio's answer is equally instructive. "So have I heard and do in part believe," he says to Marcellus, thus speaking, one feels, not just for himself but for Shakespeare and for us. *In part* believe it. At Christmas time it is hard even for the unbeliever not to believe in something if not in everything. Peace on earth, good will to men; a dream of innocence that is good to hold on to even if it is only a dream; the mystery of being a child; the possibility of hope — not even the canned carols piped out over the shopping center parking plaza from Thanksgiving on can drown it out entirely.

For a moment or two, the darkness of disenchantment, cynicism, doubt, draw back at least a little, and all the usual worldly witcheries lose something of their power to charm. Maybe we cannot manage to believe with all our hearts. But as long as the moments last, we can believe the thing most worth believing. And that may not be as far as it sounds from what belief is. For as long as the moment lasts, that hallowed, gracious time.

But no moment lasts forever, and it is not for twelve months a year that the bird of dawning singeth all night long. Darkness inevitably returns with all its shadows and ambiguities. The story of the birth of Jesus has been subjected to the most critical scrutiny by believers and unbelievers alike, and nowhere have the Nativity passages of Luke and Matthew been more rigorously and objectively analyzed than within the purview of Biblical scholarship where no fact or claim has been allowed to go unchallenged. The when, where, how of the Nativity have been for generations and continue to be the subject of endless conjecture.

Even the date of his birth is uncertain because Matthew and Luke do not agree with each other. Neither of them can be reconciled with the traditional view that he was

40 born during the first year of the Christian era as it has

come to be reckoned. Luke says he was born in the year when Cyrenius, the Roman governor of Syria, took a census of Palestine, whereas Matthew says it was during the reign of Herod the Great. The difficulty is that Cyrenius's census is known to have been taken in A.D. 6 and Herod died in 4 B.C. Thus Jesus was born either six years later than has been generally supposed or at least four years earlier. And the place of his birth is equally debatable. Bethlehem is the town traditionally named, King David's town, but that may have come about simply in order to bring history into line with the Old Testament prophecy that Bethlehem was where the Messiah as the Son of David was destined to come from. There are good reasons for believing that he may actually have been born in Nazareth.

And finally, the *how* of his birth, all the poetry that has grown up around it — the Wise Men and the Star, the shepherds keeping watch over their flocks by night and the hymn the angels sang. If someone had been there with a camera, would he have recorded any of it, or was the birth of Jesus no more if no less wonderful than any other birth? Whatever the answer, it can be based only on faith. There is no other way. The kind of objective truth a camera could have recorded is buried beneath the weight of two thousand years.

But there is of course another kind of truth. Whether he was born in 4 B.C. or A.D. 6, in Bethlehem or Nazareth, whether there were multitudes of the heavenly host to hymn the glory of it or just Mary and her husband — when the child was born, the whole course of human history was changed. That is a truth as unassailable as any truth. Art, music, literature, Western culture itself with all its institutions and Western man's whole understanding of himself

and his world — it is impossible to conceive how differently things would have turned out if that birth had not happened whenever, wherever, however it did. And there is a truth beyond that: for millions of people who have lived since, the birth of Jesus made possible not just a new way of understanding life but a new way of living it.

For better or worse, it is a truth that, for twenty centuries, there have been untold numbers of men and women who, in untold numbers of ways, have been so grasped by the child who was born, so caught up in the message

19. Holy Family. *Felt banner. Norman LaLiberté. U.S.A. contemporary.*

20. Madonna and Child Enthroned. *Sinopia, drawing for a fresco. Paolo di Stefano Badaloni. Italian, 15th century.*

he taught and the life he lived, that they have found themselves profoundly changed by their relationship with him. And they have gone on proclaiming, as the writers of the Gospels proclaimed before them, that through the birth of Jesus a life-giving power was released into the world which to their minds could have been no less than the power of God himself. This is the central truth that Matthew and Luke are trying to convey in their accounts of the Nativity. And it was a truth which no language or legend seemed too extravagant to convey. What the birth

21. The Nativity. *Pencil and crayon on paper. U.S.A. contemporary.*

meant — meant to them, to the world — was the truth that mattered to them most and, when all is said and done, perhaps the only truth that matters to anyone.

The painter sitting down at his easel, the sculptor picking up his chisel and the weaver his thread — assuming they are in it for something more than the money or the fame, it is this inward truth that they are all trying to express. You picture them at their work and try to imagine how they approached it, the fourteenth century monks and the nineteenth century Africans, the skilled ones and the

22. Adoration of the Magi. *Wooden core, silver gilt, copper gilt, enamel and filigree. Nicolas of Verdun. Mosan, 1205.*

clumsy ones, the clever ones and the ones whose cleverness was all in their fingers. For all of them, as for Mary, a kind of annunciation must have had to take place before they touched their brushes to canvas or made their first silken stitch. The Muses are only Gabriel in Grecian borrowings. Something had to stir in them asking to be given a face and a name. The task before them was to set forth in paint or gold or marble the mother and her new-born child, and one imagines that part of what they drew on was their memory of the flesh-and-blood mothers and children they

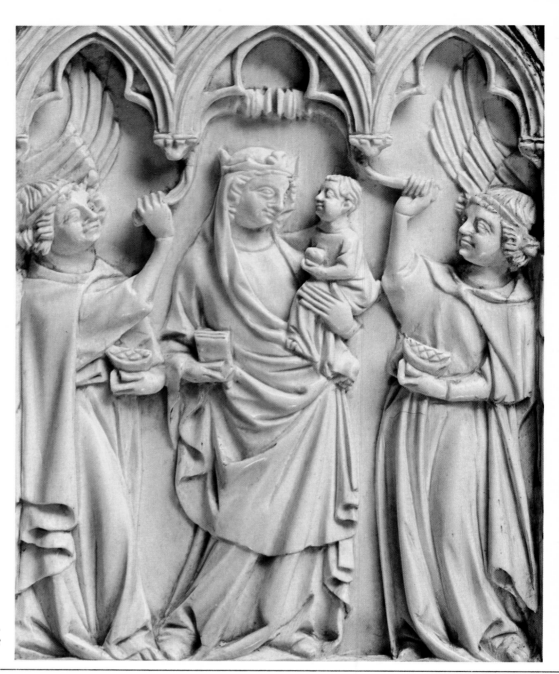

23. Standing Virgin and Child with Angels. *Ivory relief. French, second quarter of the 14th century.*

had actually seen with their own eyes — Mary as their own mother perhaps and Jesus as some child they had dandled on their own laps. But they had to dive down deeper than that presumably before they were done, down beneath memory into that shadowland finally of their own deepest and most secret desiring for a reality beyond any they had eyes to see. Thus their works of art come ultimately from the same place that prayers do, from that dimension of the self where out of their own richest silence

46

they sought to commune with Silence itself, to make themselves heard by it and to hear. Faith, said Paul, is the conviction of things not seen, and their art is their prayer to be able to see and make seen.

Without exception, the one thing that they all of them seem to have seen alike is that the Nativity was in one way or another beautiful. At first glance, that does not seem surprising. When it comes to the birth of a child, we are all of us apt to be romantics. A new life, a new hope, innocence coming into an old and weary world — if there is beauty anywhere, surely it is here. And yet Heaven knows they were also realists, most of these artists. When it comes to depicting other events in the life of Jesus, especially the events centered around his passion and death, again they saw beauty, but they saw other things too. They saw pain and contradiction, bitterness and despair. The body on the cross is a symbol of hope and innocence no less than the babe in the manger, and yet they do not shrink back from the fact that it is also a body in torment, that real blood runs down from the thorny crown, that the flesh is lacerated by scourging, the mouth open to the cry of dereliction — *My God, my God, why hast thou forsaken me* — the face of the mother disfigured by grief as she holds the corpse of her child on her knees. There is beauty too in these terrible pictures, the beauty of peace in the midst of agony, and of victory in the ashes of defeat. It is a beauty deep in shadow. But when it comes to the Nativity, there is no shadow. To portray the birth as realistically as the death is a temptation that these same masters of reality, every last one of them, was able to resist. There is no attempt to represent the throes of Mary's labor or the bloody and howling entrance of the child into the winter world. In one form or another, the manger always ap-

24. Virgin and Child Enthroned. *Serigraph.*
Sister Corita Kent. U.S.A. contemporary.

25. St. Christopher with the Christ Child,
detail. Silver, parcel gilt. French, early 15th
century.

pears as a place of beauty and holiness and never as a cold
and cheerless symbol of the world's indifference. Silent
night, holy night, all is calm, all is bright. Down through
the ages there have been countless variations on this
theme, but the theme is always the same. Not a hair of
Mary's head is out of place. The baby has been washed
and dried, the stable swept.

Glory to the new-born king. As befits the mother of a
king, Mary is dressed as a queen. She is wearing a crown,
an ivory circlet from which her mantle falls in soft, ivory

folds (23). She is carrying the child on her hip with her left hand tucked under him and her right hand holding a little book. On either side of her angels stand, and they have eyes only for her. The child too. He is smiling at his mother, but it is a smile of great deference, the kind of smile you are ready to abandon at a moment's notice if royalty is not amused, to exchange for a frown if royalty frowns. But the queen smiles. She accepts as her due that the child is trying not to make her carry his full weight. He is sitting up straight and a little precarious with one arm on her shoulder to lighten her burden as though he knows (except that he does not know, because no shadow is allowed to fall here) that the time is coming when she will have burden enough and no one to lighten it.

The child himself is not wearing his crown here, at least not yet, but elsewhere he is. He and his mother are enthroned against a background of yellow and ochre (24) where shepherds and angels, Wise Men and camels, are assembled row upon row like books on a shelf. Mary holds the infant king on her lap, and he is wearing a crown many sizes too big for him. She is holding him under his arms and his hands are raised high in the air so that we can see the suggestion of stigmata in his palms, but they are stig-mata that do not hurt, that are not wounds but only the birthmark by which the king is recognized as true king. Or the child is not wearing a crown (25) but standing up with a gown and hair of gold and flesh of silver, one hand raised in blessing and the other holding the orb of majesty as he gazes out through silver eyes at a world he already holds in the palm of his hand like the golden orb.

Even where Mary is crownless, you know her for a queen and the mother of the king by the marvelous halos she wears. Her eyes aslant, her cheeks carved round and

26. Madonna and Child. *Ivory. China.*

27. Madonna and Child. *Wood. Africa, contemporary.*

full, her eyebrows two perfect semicircles on her globed forehead, she becomes the Chinese Goddess of Mercy, Kuan Yin, in the eyes of her Chinese sculptor, and the halo he has given her petals out like a lotus (26). Only a dowager empress could wear a halo like that, could smile with such superb poise despite the loss of one arm from the elbow down. In her good arm she holds the child who is Buddha, of course, plump and inscrutable and at peace with one hand on his knee and his ankles crossed.

The halo her African sculptor gives her (27) is ribbed

28. Virgin and Child. *Oil on panel with gold overframe. Russian, 18th century.*

like the parasol carried over the head of a Congo king. Her ceremonial headdress comes to a point in front like a unicorn's horn, and she sits barefoot and stiff as the tree she is carved from, paralyzed with the holiness of her high office and the sacredness of the black and holy child. His head is covered with tight black wool, and she cradles it in one hand. He is asleep with one arm folded back across his mother's wooden breast where her heart has all but stopped beating from the awesomeness and honor of

the thing.

But it is left for Russian Orthodoxy to give her the most imperial halo of them all, a great Ferris wheel freighted with seraphim and seashells, with flowers and flames and the sacred monograms of herself and her son. Even her czarina's crown is (28) lost in the crazy golden carnival of it, and certainly her face is. Her face is the blazing wheel's still, gray hub. Saddened and wearied by the magnificent tastelessness of it all, she supports her cheek in one hand, her fingers delicately crooked out to shield her eyes from the wheeling light. Her son's face is grayer and more remote still. There are circles under his eyes as he reads his Cyrillic scroll in her arms. Wearing scarlet and gold, they have both become prisoners in their own glory.

But if there is the beauty of what is majestic and powerful, there is the beauty also of what is humble and powerless. Like any child, Jesus as a child has one power only and that is the power to love and be loved which is of all powers the most powerful, because it alone can conquer the human heart; at the same time it is of all powers the most powerless, because it can do nothing except by consent. It is of the very essence of love to leave us free to respond or not to respond because the moment it attempts to force our hand, it is no longer love but coercion, and what it elicits from us is no longer love but obedience. The greatest single argument against the existence of God is the presence of evil in the world, and to the degree that the Christian Faith attempts to answer it, its answer is all tied up in this. The argument is simply stated: if there is a God who is both good and all-powerful, why do terrible things happen in the world? Why does God allow men to murder and wage wars? Why does he allow them to remain indifferent to each other's needs so that the poor go uncared for and children starve and in a sense all of us go hungry if

29. Virgin and Child. *Oil on canvas. Korea, 20th century.*

only for the peace and understanding that the world cannot give? If there is a God, why did he not with his great
goodness make things right in the first place, or why does
he not with his great power intervene in the affairs of the
world to make things right at least in the second place,
now? What Christianity in effect seems to say is that God
could presumably do these things — could have turned us
out perfectly as an engineer turns out a perfect machine or
could step in when we get out of line and move us around
like pawns on a chessboard. But as Christianity under-

55

30. Nativity. *Oil on canvas. Koseki. Korea, 20th century.*

stands it, God does not want us related to him as a machine to an engineer or pawns to a cosmic kibitzer. He wants us related to him as children are related to their father. He wants us in other words to love him, and if our love is to be spontaneous and real, we must be free also not to love him with all its grim consequences of human suffering. Evil exists in the world not because God is indifferent or powerless or absent but because man is free, and free he must be if he is to love freely, free he must be if he is to be human.

56

31. Nativity. *Oil on canvas. American, early 19th century.*

This is part at least of what many of the other Nativity scenes seem to be saying. Like any baby, Jesus as a baby does not judge or exhort or puzzle the world with his teaching. He makes no demands, threatens no punishment, offers no rewards. The world is free to take him or leave him. He belongs no more to the three kings who bring him their expensive gifts than to the cattle who only watch him in silence through their great moist eyes, and neither kings nor cattle belong any more to him than the other. Mary is no longer the Queen of Heaven in these,

but only Mary; and Jesus is no longer the child-king who already rules the world from his mother's lap but, like any child, is himself at the mercy of the world.

The dove of the Holy Ghost has become a pet white bird that perches on his finger (29) in a Korean painting where Mary and Jesus are both too pretty in their silk kimonos, their expressions too sweet. Or the manger has become a velvet-lined sewing basket (30) with a picture post card winter scene visible through the window and a mother and child who look as though they have less of deity about them than of Disney. In trying to say too much, piety always runs the risk of saying too little or saying it wrong, and the great pitfall of Christian art, especially when it tries to portray the birth of Christ, is sentimentalism, the attempt to evoke more feeling in us than even God can feel. The crèche (31) becomes a painted backdrop, the floor a carpeted stage, the manger a prop lined with artificial straw. It is an opera set with the Magi robed in costumes left over from *L'Amore dei Tre Re*, their halos having the effect of a spotlight from the proscenium arch. The Madonna is a diva cuddling a wax doll. Two rustic boys hold flutes to their lips and behind them a bearded shepherd raises one arm. He is singing Gounod's *Ave Maria* as Joseph, a basso, waits to make his entrance from the wings. Neither the holiness nor the humanness of the moment is rendered here so much as the schmaltz, and the manufacturers of Christmas cards have taken their cues from these, translating the event into *tableaux vivants* so idealized and bogus that we can exchange them without committing ourselves to anything.

What saves the day is particularity, the ability of the artist to fasten on some detail that rings like truth. In a thirteenth century ivory (32) the wryly precocious child

32. Seated Virgin and Child. Ivory. French, late 13th century.

33. Madonna and Child Enthroned. *Tempera on panel. Ethiopia, 20th century.*

34. Virgin and Child. *Wood polychromed. Melanesia.*

reaches up to chuck his mother under the chin; and her indulgent smile, as she recoils from him slightly, escapes bathos, because the artist has seen them both as a kind of joke, which of course they are — the whole idea of incarnation as a kind of vast joke whereby the creator of the ends of the earth comes among us in diapers. "A stumbling block to Jews and folly to gentiles," Paul called it in his letter to the Corinthians, and until we too have taken the idea of the God-man seriously enough to be scandalized by it, we have not taken it as seriously as it demands to be taken.

Mary nurses the child at her breast (33), and her breast is round and full as a birthday balloon and the child's eyes sleepy and out of focus as he suckles it, his feet dangling down in high-heeled pumps. It is the great wineskin of a breast that points to the scandal here: that the Word made flesh hunger as any flesh hungers, and although there is somebody to feed him now, someday there may be nobody. He has given us the power one way or another to destroy him, if that is our pleasure — this ultimate reach of our freedom.

No one sees the peril of the child better than the Melanesian primitive who carved it out of wood and painted it. Mary is naked to the waist with gold bracelets on her arms and a gold choker. She wears a terra cotta cap. Her pendulous breasts hang flat. She is almost chinless with a long nose and heavy lips drawn down. She is looking straight ahead through glazed eyes, her black irises surrounded on all sides with white. But it is the child who sees most clearly what is going to become of him. He clings to her like a monkey, his cheek pressed tight against her breast. He is naked except for a gold belt, and his scrawny buttocks jut out over his mother's wrist. His jaw is clenched, and he is staring out, bug-eyed, at something his mother has not yet seen. He is literally scared stiff (34).

35. Virgin and Child. *Enamel plaque. France, Limoges, 15th century.*

If ever, contrary to what has been said, the Nativity is represented in shadow, the shadow is reflected here in the terrified eyes of this marmoset of a child. If the awesome price man pays for his freedom to love is the freedom also not to love with all its attendant suffering, then, what the terror of the child tells us is, that this is the price that God also must pay. The God who is in the black child is destined to suffer not just at the hands of the loveless world but also for its sake. "He who loves a hundred has a

36. The Flight into Egypt. *Serigraph. Sadao Watanabe. Japan, 1970.*

hundred woes. He who loves ten has ten woes. He who loves none has no woes," says Buddha, and therefore in place of love Buddha enjoins his followers to a kind of impersonal and invulnerable benevolence. But the God who is in Jesus loves no matter what the cost because that is the innermost secret of his nature, and he enjoins all men to do likewise because it is also the innermost secret of theirs. Buddhism and Christianity agree that to love is to suffer, because wherever the ones we love suffer, our love suffers with them and for them; but whereas Buddhism

64

37. The Flight into Egypt. *Painting on glass. Austria, 18th century.*

says that this suffering is above all things to be avoided, Christianity says that it is above all things to be embraced, because it is by suffering in love for one another that we can help work each other's redemption and our own too, thus participating in the redemptive activity of God himself. It is a high and holy way that men are called to follow, and its end is wholeness and peace, but there are many dark miles ahead for those who follow it and for none more than for this child who must not only lead the

65 way but be the way. He does well to cling in terror to his

mother's breast.

In a fifteenth century French enamel (35), against a blue sky spangled with stars, what he clings to is the cross, and not a gold cross or a jeweled one this time, not the cross as ritual object, but a T-shaped wooden cross that has been made to be used, a cross with nails in place where the hands and feet will go. The face of the child is not frightened here, but it is old before its time, the eyes already dead a little, with shadows under them.

And yet . . . Silent night, holy night. All is calm, all is bright. It is the calm before the storm, but it is no less calm for that, no less beautiful. It is beauty in one form or another that they are all trying to convey whether they make the child white or black, fat or thin, playful or pensive, picture-book pretty or a little old man, whether his mother is the Queen of Heaven or only the carpenter's wife. If shadows are to intrude upon the brightness of his birth, they must be only the shadows of shadows, visible only in the mark on a hand or the look in an eye. It is as if they are saying that the time will come soon enough to sorrow with him as the Man of Sorrows, and in the meanwhile it is enough that we rejoice in him as the Princeling of Peace. As long as he stays the babe in the manger, he asks us nothing harder than to love him and accept his love, and the temptation is thus to keep him a babe forever, for our sakes and for his sake too. Hence, perhaps, the inevitable stillness of these paintings and carvings. Nothing moves. The very air is gold and unstirring, the angels caught like birds in a net. Time itself seems to have stopped, and the whole creation holds its breath as if for fear that otherwise time will start again and with it the long journey the child must take through time and the faithful with him. As long as he is young, he seems to stand still,

38. The Flight into Egypt. *Oil on canvas. Ivo Dulčič. Yugoslavia, 1916.*

39. St. Christopher and the Christ Child. *Oil on canvas. Otto Dix. Germany, 20th century.*

40. St. Christopher and the Christ Child, *detail of the child Jesus. Oil on canvas. Otto Dix. Germany, 20th century.*

beyond the reach of time and its lengthening shadows.

For instance, when an angel appeared to Joseph in a dream and warned him of the wrath of Herod, Joseph took his wife and child to Egypt, but it is no furtive flight of refugees, no grim escape from the tyrant's sword. Mary and Jesus ride a donkey, and Joseph walks beside them (36, 37, 38). Mary is wearing her good clothes although in most versions she seems to have left her halo behind. Maybe it was an attempt to remain incognito or just her hurry to leave. Joseph is walking with a staff because he

41. Jesus Among the Doctors. *Wood, poly-chromed relief. Germany, Naumburg, 15th century.*

is not getting any younger, and the baby is bundled up against the fresh air. It is a family holiday, a trip to the country, and if there is trouble ahead, it is a long way ahead. The sky is blue, and the baby has fallen asleep.

The same note is struck in a German painting of another journey, this time an entirely legendary one (39). Saint Christopher is carrying the child across a raging stream, and the deeper in he wades, the heavier the child becomes until finally he cries out, "Had I borne the whole world on my shoulders, the burden had not been heavier!" to which

70

42. The Holy Family. *Painting on silk.
Japan, 20th century.*

the child replies, "Christopher, thou hast not only borne all the world upon thee, but thou hast borne him that created the world and must bear the heaviness of its sin upon his shoulders." It is a dark word the child speaks and a dark journey he is embarked upon, but as with the Flight into Egypt, the child is untouched by the darkness of it because again time has stopped, and the child we see is a child who for the moment is beyond the power of time to hurt. He rides the old saint's back like a child on a pony.

71 Blond and blue-eyed, a perfect Aryan, he wears a golden

43. The Holy Family, *detail of the Christ Child.* Painted on glass. Austrian, contemporary.

gown and stands in a halo as warm and bright as summer. He raises his hand to bless a world whose fateful heaviness he has yet to feel.

When he was twelve, Luke says, Mary and Joseph took him to Jerusalem for the Passover, and somewhere in the confusion they lost him. When they finally found him three days later, he was in the Temple deep in debate with the venerable teachers of the Law. These were the very men who were to become his archenemies in days to come — the pillars of orthodoxy who were to see him as a threat to everything they held most sacred — but at this point they were all admiration, "astonished at his understanding and answers." It is a very Jewish story — our son the theologian, the parents' discreet but fathomless pride in the accomplishments of their first-born. You can see it in Mary's face (41), in the way Joseph scratches his head in wonderment, in the rapt attention of the elders themselves, one of whom is checking out the boy's answers in a copy of the Torah. And you can see how proud the boy is too. He is perched on top of a ladder so that his head is higher than any of them, and his face is the face of the wise child who knows his father. "Wist ye not that I must be about my Father's business?" he asks, and he does not have a doubt in the world who that Father is. He will return to Jerusalem another day. The ladder he sits on will become the ladder his executioners climb to nail him to the cross, and the old men will be the ones who hand him over to them. But time has stopped on its way to that time, and they are all of them caught like flies in amber in the proud peace of this first encounter.

When they get back to Nazareth, the cherry trees are in bloom (42). The bay beyond the garden fence is calm and the grass is green with spring. Mary is out in the sunshine spinning at her wheel. In a blue kimono Joseph is at his carpentry. He has one knee on a two-by-four to hold it steady while he saws it. His son is walking toward him wearing white trousers, red tunic, and clogs. On his shoulder he is carrying a piece of wood. Do not think for a moment, the painter says, that what he is carrying on his shoulder has anything to do with what he will someday be famous for carrying, or if you must think of it, let it be for a moment only. He is carrying wood to make a pagoda out of or a cage for Chinese nightingales. Whatever moments

JESUS HAPPY
AND
SAD

are to come, this moment is forever. Nothing that will come to be can make this moment otherwise.

It can be sentimentality, prettiness, unreality, but it can be something else too, this thing that all these representations of the birth and childhood of Jesus are saying, sometimes in spite of themselves and sometimes the shallowest of them as well as the deepest. Everything that ever happens in a life goes on being a part of that life, not just the thing that happens last. The man on the cross is also the babe in the manger, the child on his journeys, the boy in the Temple. No man is such a prisoner of chronology but that his past and his future too are not a living part of his present, accessible to him in his dreams if nowhere else and accessible to us in our dreams about him. "Before Abraham was, I am," Jesus said. Before my time on earth ran out, I am on earth and this time is my time. Before darkness covered the whole land and the veil of the Temple was rent, all is calm, all is bright. Before I was a man, I am a child, a God.

Not first the birth, and then the life, and then the death, but all three of them together, all three of them always impinging upon us at once. Let the last word about the child be a child's word (44): JESUS HAPPY AND SAD, those lopsided letters scrawled out above the lopsided child with his shoulders hunched against the world and his arms stiff and self-conscious at his sides. He has a clown's face with a clown's broad and crooked smile. He has all of his life ahead of him and behind him too. If eternity is not endless time but the essence of all times combined, past, present and future, then it is in eternity that he stands. The D of SAD hovers near him like the bird of dawning that singeth all night long. One eye is shoe-button bright. The other streams with tears.

44. Jesus Happy and Sad. *Tempera on paper. Maura Cronin, age 4. U.S.A.*

75

"Glory to the newborn King"

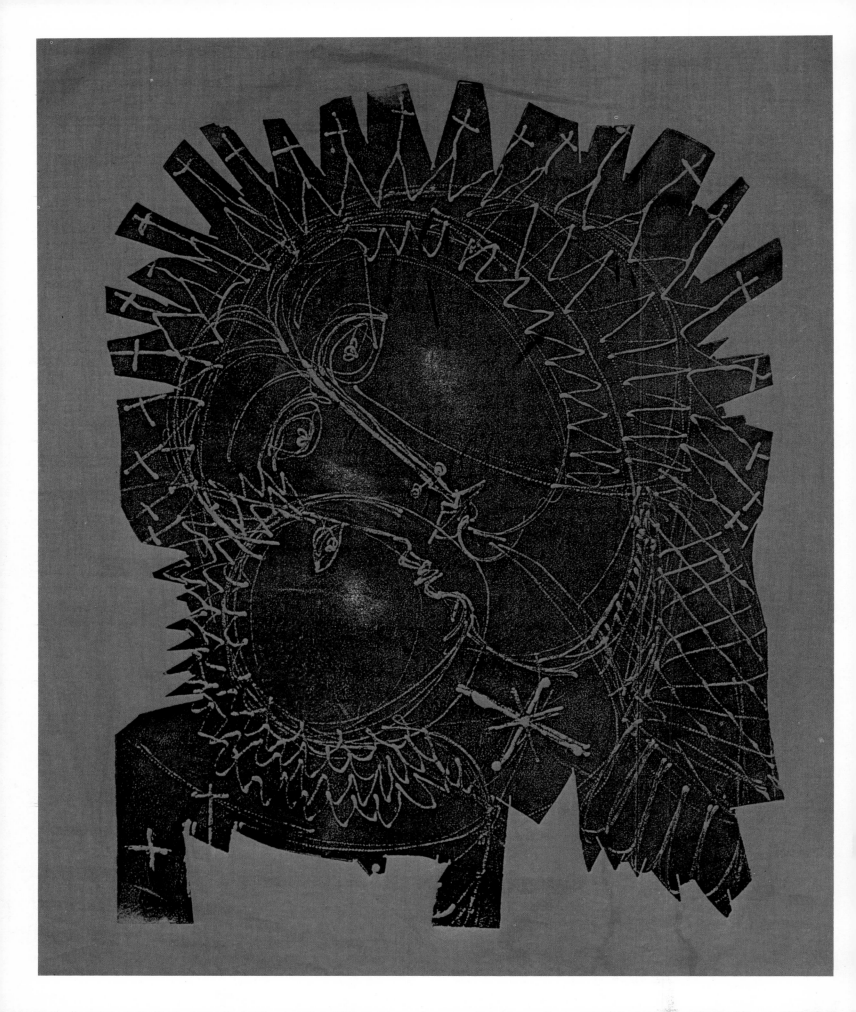

51. The Raising of Lazarus. *Champlevé enamel. Châsse of St. Mark. France, about 1210-1230.*

MINISTRY

PRECEEDING PAGE

50. The Baptism of Christ, *detail of Christ. Polychromed wood relief. Germany, Franconia, late 15th century.*

"Jesus, when he began his ministry, was about thirty years of age," Luke says. He is no longer the kingly child enthroned high above the world's power to do him harm and beyond the touch of time. The angels who attended his birth have vanished, and the Magi have long since left their gifts at his feet and gone home. The star of Bethlehem has faded from view in the light of the hot, near-Eastern sun. If the shepherds who kept watch over their flocks by night were once convinced that he was the Long Expected One, the One by whom heaven and earth are named, they give no signs of remembering. The child has become a man, and, like all men, is caught up in time, in change and mortality. To understand him, we must understand the time he moved in and that moved in him. The difficulty is that this is just what we cannot do very satisfactorily.

Facts and figures abound, but what it was like to be a product of that distant time, to think as men thought then, to believe as they believed, to know no more and no less than they knew, is beyond our power because just as they were captives of their time, so we are captives of ours.

Palestine was a province of the Roman Empire which allowed the Jews a measure of self-rule but maintained a strong military presence and kept them under close supervision. The Jews were divided into various sects. There were the Zealots, the fire-breathing nationalists who looked for the expulsion of Rome and the restoration of Jewish independence. There were semi-monastic sects like the Essenes who retreated to the wilderness around the Dead Sea in an effort to turn the clock back to the time of Israel's purity when life was comparatively simple and uncomplicated. There were the Pharisees who sought to reinterpret the ancient Law of Moses to meet the exigencies of a situation that had changed profoundly since Moses' day, and the Scribes, the scholars who worked out these reinterpretations which were eventually to become as binding as the Law. There were the ultra-conservative Sadducees who tended to shut their eyes to change in general and refused to reinterpret anything. What was good enough for Moses was good enough for them, and whereas the Pharisees believed in the resurrection of the dead, the Sadducees rejected it because it was not to be found in Scripture. There were the *Am-Ha'ares*, or People of the Land, the unlettered commonality who did not so much hold views as they were simply swayed by them — sometimes one, sometimes another — and whose main business was just to survive as best they could the continual onslaughts of poverty and disease.

In all of these groups hope ran high that God would send a Messiah to redeem his chosen people, Israel, but this hope took many different forms, themselves indistinct and overlapping. Some dreamed that the Messiah would come as a warrior like King David to throw off the yoke of foreign rule. Others thought of him as a great priest like Melchizedek or a great prophet like Elijah. Somehow Jesus

52. Christ Cleansing the Temple. *Oil on panel. El Greco (Domenico Theotokopoulos). Italy, about 1570.*

88

was a part of all this and all this a part of him, but no one can say just how or to what effect.

The writers of the Gospels make no attempt to show how he fitted into the religio-political complexities of first century Israel but only how he fitted into the hearts of those who believed in him. They make no attempt either to depict his personality, to suggest the way he walked, talked, the kind of things that made him laugh, his attitude toward his friends, his family. There are only hints of these matters, to be read differently by each who reads them.

There seems to be a kind of sad humor about some of his parables — the man who tries to sleep through his friend's importunate midnight knocking; the rich man trying to squeeze into Paradise like a camel through a needle's eye — and one can imagine him smiling as he told them, but maybe the smile is only one's own. What seems to have made him angriest was hypocrisy and irrelevance, and thus it is the Pharisees who come in for his strongest attacks, the good people who should have known better. "You brood of vipers," he called them. "How can you speak good when you are evil?" When news was brought him that his friend Lazarus was dead, we are told that he wept, and at Gethsemane on the night of his arrest, the prospect of his own death shook him as it would shake any man. He sweated blood, the Gospels tell us, and prayed God to take the bitter cup from him if it was his will.

But there seem to have been happy moments too, though the Gospels do not make much of them — the wedding at Cana where he saved the day by turning water into wine, the time he was out with the disciples on the

Sea of Galilee and was lulled asleep by the rocking of the

boat. Unlike John the Baptist, he was no grim ascetic but was accused of being a glutton and a drunk; and when the disciples of John asked him why he and his disciples did not fast, his answer was, "Can the wedding guests mourn as long as the bridegroom is with them?"

The author of the Epistle to the Hebrews describes him as "one who in every respect has been tempted as we are yet without sinning" — tempted to be a demagogue, a spellbinder, a mere humanitarian, we are told in the account of his encounter in the wilderness with Satan, who offered him all the kingdoms of the earth if he would only settle for them and no more; tempted to escape martyrdom as Peter urged him to, saying, "God forbid, Lord. This shall never happen to you," to which Jesus replied, "Get behind me, Satan. You are a hindrance to me;" tempted, ultimately, to doubt the very faithfulness of God as he howls out his *Eloi, Eloi* from the cross.

And yet without sinning, Hebrews says. However great the temptation to abandon once and for all both his fellowmen and his God — who together he had good reason to believe had abandoned him — he never ceased to reach out to them in love, forgiving finally his own executioners. He addressed his cry of dereliction to a God who, in spite of everything, he believed to the end was near enough, and counted him dear enough, to hear it. The paradoxical assertion that Jesus was both fully man and in some way also fully God seems to many the unnecessary and obfuscating doctrine of later theologians, but the truth of the matter is that like all doctrines it was an experience first, in this case the experience of the simple men who had actually known him. Having talked with him and eaten with him, having seen him angry, sad, merry, tired, and

91

Jesus Calmings The Sea

Curtis Aurenne St. Aloysius

53. Jesus Calming the Sea. *Crayon on paper. Curtis Aurenne, age 10. U.S.A., contemporary.*

finally dead, they had no choice but to say that he was a man even as they themselves were men. But having found in him an undying power to heal and transform their lives, they had no choice but to say that he was God too if only because there was no other way of saying it.

If the doctrine of the divinity of Christ is paradoxical, it is only because the experience was paradoxical first. Much as we may wish it otherwise, reality seldom comes to us simple, logical, all of a piece. Man is an animal, we must say if we are honest, but he is also more than animal.

54. Christ on Lake Gennesaret. *Oil on canvas. Eugène Delacroix. France, early 19th century.*

In honesty we must say that too. If we are determined to speak the plain sense of our experience, we must be willing to risk the charge of speaking what often sounds like nonsense.

What we see of this extraordinary man we see only dimly and at the remove of centuries from a time we can never fully understand. Yet to read the New Testament with not just our eyes but our hearts and imagination open as well is to catch a glimpse of a figure who from time to time we believe we are finally able to identify whether as

93

Gentle Jesus Meek and Mild or Christ the Tiger, the teacher, the revolutionary, the merchant of dreams.

But even when we think we have come close to seeing him for whom he truly was — the figure he cut, the face he wore — we must acknowledge always that what we have seen does not at most include who he was behind that face, the mystery of his inner life, of how he thought of himself and how he would have thought of us.

Did he think of himself as the Messiah, for instance? Some have argued that he did not, pointing to, among other things, what is often his curious ambivalence when the question is put to him directly. "Are you the one who is to come, or shall we look for another?" the disciples of John the Baptist ask him. To which his answer is, "Go and tell John what you hear and see," and when Pilate says, "Tell us if you are the Christ, the Son of God," his reply, according to Matthew, is the equally cryptic "You have said so."

On the other hand, it is possible that he was reluctant to accept the title simply because it was charged with chauvinistic associations from which he wished to disassociate himself. Mark, in any event, has Jesus answer Pilate's question with an unequivocal "I am," and it is hard to see why they would have crucified him as a self-proclaimed Messiah with "Jesus of Nazareth, King of the Jews" nailed up over his head in three languages unless he had indeed proclaimed it. And it is hard to believe that his followers would have gone on proclaiming it about him unless they had had it in some sense from his own lips. But even if that is true, it still leaves the question, In what sense? If he thought of himself as the Messiah, what kind of Messiah did he have in mind?

55. The Raising of Lazarus, *detail, head of Christ. Stone. Cathedral. England, Chichester, 13th century.*

One thing at least seems clear. His role as he understood it was not to lead men in glory but to suffer for them in love. "The Son of Man came not to be served but to serve," he said, "and to give his life as a ransom for many." Again and again he strikes this note. The road that God has set before him is a road that involves great suffering, and suffering is to be the lot as well of all who choose to follow him on it. He makes no bones about this. "If any man would come after me, let him deny himself and take up his cross and follow me," he tells his disciples. And when

95

a woman asks him to assure her sons places of prominence in Heaven, he turns to them and asks, "Are you able to drink the cup that I am to drink?" If the guilty are to be saved, it is only by the suffering for them of the innocent, of the Messiah himself as the innocent one who shoulders the burden of their guilt.

Somewhere in the background of this there seems to stand a shadowy figure out of the Book of Isaiah known as the Suffering Servant who is described in one of a series of poems as "despised and rejected of men, a man of sorrows and acquainted with grief," as one who "was wounded for our transgressions and bruised for our iniquities" so that "with his stripes we are healed." The Gospels contain a number of echoes from these ancient poems including the opening words of Mark and the words spoken at the time of Jesus' baptism. Jesus' own view of himself seems to have been unmistakably influenced by them as when, on his return to the synagogue at Nazareth, the passage he chooses to read is from them: "The Spirit of the Lord is upon me because the Lord has anointed me to bring good tidings to the poor; he has sent me to bind up the brokenhearted, to proclaim liberty to the captives and recovering of sight to the blind."

The poor, the brokenhearted, the disinherited, the riff-raff — from the beginning of his ministry these were the ones that Jesus particularly addressed himself to rather than to the ones who would have given him a more powerful following. Nothing he ever said strikes deeper chords than "Come unto me all you who labor and are heavy laden, and I will give you rest," not that in a sense all men are not one way or another laboring and heavy laden under the burden of their own lives but that it is the down-

56. Jesus Healing the Sick. *Oil on canvas. Christian Wilhelm Ernst Dietrich. Germany, 17th century.*

trodden, the outcasts, who understand it best and are most apt to prick up their ears at the sound of his words. The rich, the respectable, the resourceful are tempted always to believe that they have no burden they cannot manage well enough on their own. It was the riffraff he spoke to, the riffraff who became his followers, his disciples even — tax collectors, whores, hicks — and when the Pharisees took him to task for this, his answer was "Those who are well have no need of a physician, but those who are sick," and then "I came not to call the righteous but sinners."

97

And call them to what? What was the thrust of the message he carried, this strange and elusive man whom we can never either really know or escape knowing? What was the gospel, God's spiel, good news he gave his life to proclaiming, not just to Jews because "many shall come from the east and the west," as he told the Roman centurion, "and shall sit down with Abraham and Isaac and Jacob in the Kingdom of Heaven"?

To everybody who would listen then, what was his holy pitch? Not like the prophets, who always produced their credentials by telling the story of how God called them to be prophets in the first place and who always covered themselves by prefacing their words with "thus saith the Lord;" and not like the rabbis, who cited Scriptural chapter and verse for everything they said; but with an utter and unqualified conviction of his power to speak on his own authority of even the highest and holiest things, he proclaimed the Kingdom of God.

He said the Kingdom was coming, a new order of things in which God's will was to be done on earth as it was done in Heaven so that at last men would love their neighbors as themselves and God as their father. He said it was coming soon and was indeed already partly present in his own healing work of proclaiming it. He said that there was nothing men could do either to hasten it or prevent it but that they were to work for it, pray for it, and above all be ready to receive it when the time came.

In his own way, John the Baptist had proclaimed something like this before him, but whereas John had proclaimed it as a prophet of doom using images like a threshing floor and a fan, or an axe ready to strike, and telling men they had to repent or else, Jesus proclaimed it as God's good gift which would be given whether men repented or not and pictured the experience of entering it as an experience of joy like attending a great feast or stumbling on buried treasure or finding a pearl of great price. This was what made his good news good and also what made it new, this message from the stars that it was not just to the righteous that the Kingdom would come but to any man however sinful who would only open his heart to receive it.

You did not have to make yourself righteous first in order to qualify for admission — in fact by their very effort to fulfill the letter of the Law, the Pharisees were continually missing its spirit — but if you would only accept the gift of God's love in humility and faith, God himself would make you loving which was, Jesus said, the fulfillment of all the Law and the prophets.

Thus it was not by being good that man was to be saved, because by himself that was just what man could not be. And when the rich young ruler called Jesus "good teacher," Jesus himself bridled under the epithet saying, "Why do you call me good? No one is good but God alone." It was not by good works that man had to win his way into the Kingdom, but like the Prodigal Son all he had to do was set his face for home and God would be there to welcome him with open arms before he even had a chance to ask forgiveness for all the years of his prodigality.

But if good works are not the cause of salvation, they are nonetheless the mark and effect of it. If the forgiven man does not become forgiving, the loved man loving, then he is only deceiving himself. "You shall know them by their fruits," Jesus says, and here Gentle Jesus Meek and Mild becomes Christ the Tiger, becomes both at once, this stern and loving man. "Every tree that does not bear good fruit is cut down and thrown into the fire," he says, and Saint Paul is only echoing him when he writes to the Galatians, "The fruit of the Spirit is love, joy, peace, patience, kindness, goodness, faithfulness, gentleness, self-control; against such there is no law."

This then is the gospel that Jesus seems both to have proclaimed with his lips and lived with his life, not just preaching to the dispossessed of his day from a high pulpit, but coming down and acting it out by giving himself to them body and soul as if he actually enjoyed it — horrifying all Jericho by spending the night there not with the local rabbi, say, or some prominent Pharisee but with Zaccheus of all people, the crooked tax collector. When Simon the Pharisee laid into him for letting a streetwalker dry his feet with her hair, Jesus said, "I tell you her sins, which are many, are forgiven, for she loved much." It is no wonder that from the very start of his ministry the forces of Jewish morality and of Roman law were both out to get him because to him the only morality that mattered was the one that sprang from the forgiven heart like fruit from the well-watered tree, and the only law he acknowledged as ultimate was the law of love.

57. Christ Entering Jerusalem on an Ass. Linden wood, polychromed. Germany, Bavaria, 15th century.

A man who was of all men most human yet like no man seems to have seen himself as divine. A man of sorrows who at the end of his life said, "These things I have spoken to you that my joy may be in you and that your joy may be full." A man who ate and drank and wept with sinners but who lashed out against sin with a violence that can still make the blood run cold; who was tempted to fall but never fell; who went down in defeat only to rise up in

100 victory — it is no wonder that we can never fully know

him or be sure even of what little we think we do know, including the content of these pages. As Albert Schweitzer wrote at the end of *The Quest of the Historical Jesus*, "He come to us as One unknown, without a name, as of old, by the lakeside, He came to those men who knew Him not. He speaks to us the same word: 'Follow thou me!' and sets us to the tasks which He has to fulfil for our time. He commands. And to those who obey Him, whether they be wise or simple, He will reveal Himself in the toils, the conflicts, the sufferings, which they shall pass through in His fellowship, and, as an ineffable mystery, they shall learn in their own experience Who He is."

Follow thou me. In their own way the artists too try to follow that command and with the tools of their trade on their backs seek to follow him deep enough to catch at least a glimpse of that face that changed the face of all subsequent history including their own. A fifteenth century German woodcarver follows him as far as the banks of the Jordan where John the Baptist sees him coming and says, "Behold, the Lamb of God, who takes away the sin of the world."

The face of Jesus (57) is pale as ivory, only his cheeks flushed and feverish, as he awaits the cleansing water. "I need to be baptized by you," John says, but Jesus answers, "Let it be so now, for thus it is fitting;" and as he answers, his lips part in a smile of profound gaiety as though at the absurdity of the one who takes away the sin of the world receiving on his own head the baptism of repentance for the forgiveness of sins.

Or perhaps it is the smile of the Renaissance prince who receives at the hands of a vassal a gift which in his great wealth he does not need but which he more than pays for

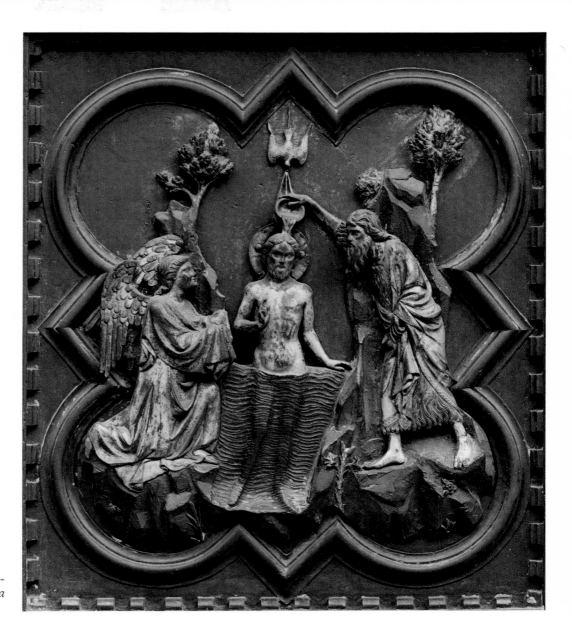

58. The Baptism of Christ. *Gilt bronze relief. Baptistery doors, south side. Andrea Pisano. Italy, Florence, about 1330.*

by the exquisite courtesy with which he is pleased to accept it. Thus it is *fitting*, he says. Or maybe it is the smile of a man who at the start of a journey which he knows will end in his death shows by his smiling how he knows too that the death he journeys to is as nothing compared with the life that will spring from it like wheat from a buried seed. His teeth show even and white as seeds between his red lips. His glance is sideways, inward, as though something buried deep within himself is already inching slowly toward the sun.

59. The Calling of Peter and Paul. *Serigraph. Sadao Watanabe. Japan, 1970.*

In Florence a hundred years earlier, Andrea Pisano (58) rendered the same moment in bronze on the great south doors of the Baptistery because the moment itself was a door. The Baptism in Jordan was the door through which Jesus passed into his ministry because it seems to have been at this moment that he first knew himself fully to be the Anointed One, which is what *messiah* means in Hebrew, *christos* in Greek.

Gathering his camel's hair garment at the knee to keep
104 it from getting wet, John pours the water on his head from

60. The Marriage at Cana. *Ivory plaque from the archepiscopal throne of Maximianus. Early Christian, 545-553.*

61. The Miracle of the Loaves and the Fishes. *Lithograph. Jean Heiberg. U.S.A., contemporary.*

a chalice as the Holy Spirit descends upon Jesus like a dove, and a voice from Heaven, echoing the first of the Suffering Servant poems, says, "Thou art my beloved son; with thee I am well pleased." Jesus seems to have broken with John at some later date, not baptizing his followers as John did, but from the earliest stages of the Christian movement, the sacrament was reinstituted as a symbol of dying to the old and rising to the new, thus becoming the door through which all believers must pass.

106   If in the scenes of his birth and childhood Jesus seems

to be always standing still on the banks of time which never touches him, in these scenes of his ministry he is caught up in the relentless flow of it. If there are moments of repose now, they are moments salvaged in the midst of turbulent activity. One pictures him continually moving forward, continually speaking, as though he knows that there is no moment to lose.

He is passing along by the Sea of Galilee when he sees Andrew and Peter casting their nets into the water; and without preface or explanation he calls out to them on the run, "Follow me, and I will make you become fishers of men," as they rise to their feet in their small green boat, and one of them reaches out to take his hand. White and yellow water lilies bob against the green hull, and the air is full of fish. They all three wear chin whiskers (59), and their faces are grave and simian, the bodies of the disciples tense as they prepare to leap to the shore to follow him.

With the jerky haste of an old newsreel, Jesus flickers across the light-struck Galilean landscape. Parables and beatitudes fill the air about him like scratches on an old film — Blessed are the meek, the poor, the pure in heart — and people throng about him to be healed. A woman stretches out her hand to touch the hem of his garment as he goes hurrying by. At Cana he stops long enough to go to a wedding, and when his mother tells him the wine has given out, his answer is impatient and time haunted. "My hour has not yet come," he says, but he takes time to do her bidding anyway and makes wine out of the six great jars of water. He leans (60) wearily on his staff with all the long miles still ahead of him and not even here a chance to forget. The steward of the feast holds his goblet in one hand and with the other makes an expansive gesture as he

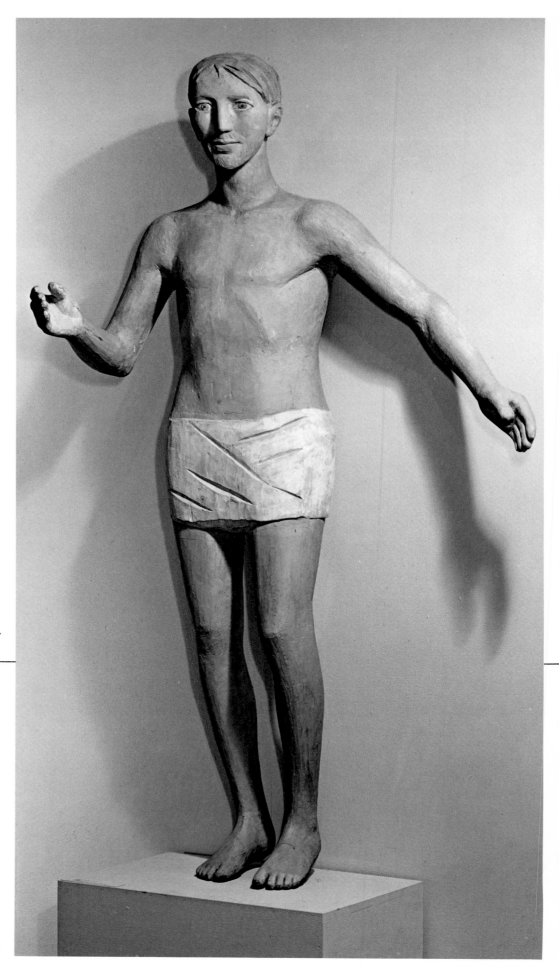

62. Christ. *Painted wood. Ivar Lindekrantz.*
Sweden, contemporary.

108

63. Christ and the Samaritan Woman at the Well. *Painted and gilded glass. German, early 15th century.*

smiles like a connoisseur and congratulates the bridegroom on having saved the best wine for the last. The face of Jesus is unsmiling, his head tilted to the side and his eyes closed like a traveler who is dead for sleep.

Somewhere, against a sky of larkspur blue (61), he stands in an orange robe holding a basket of bread. A child who barely comes up to his waist stands in front of him grabbing up for the bread as if his life depends on it, which of course it does. Jesus' eyes are dazed and faraway. He

seems to have forgotten where he is, but the child's little

comic strip mouth is open as he tries to remind him. Soon, like a man waking up out of a dream, Jesus will lower the basket to where the child can pillage it.

Jesus is blond and young (62). He is naked except for a white cloth wrapped around his loins. His body is handsome and lithe as a swimmer's. He is poised on the brink of something so extraordinary that he looks almost hypnotized by it. His stare is intensely expectant, and there is a controlled jubilance about his lips. He has his right hand extended in front of him as though either to offer help or to beseech it, and with his left arm extended out to the side he seems to be balancing himself like a tightrope walker as he prepares to step forward. His heart is in his mouth. Whatever it is that he is about to do, it is a matter of life and death or possibly both.

In Samaria he stops at a well (63) because he is tired and thirsty from his journeying. There is a woman drawing water. She is dressed in the height of Renaissance fashion with a modish turban on her head and pointed slippers on her feet. The bodice of her gown is cut low, and she has one knee raised to display a slender ankle. The impression the artist gives is that Jesus did not have to be clairvoyant to see her for what she was. She is as transparent as the glass she is painted on, but she does not seem to mind being seen through. She could be the Wife of Bath the way she does her frisky little jig there with the rope in her hands to raise the bucket.

The two disciples who are lurking in the background are clearly dismayed by her unseemly behavior — one of them plucks at his beard and the other averts his frowning gaze — but Jesus wastes no time on moral exhortation. Since their paths may never cross again, he must speak to her of what matters most while he still has the chance. "Every one who drinks of this water will thirst again," he tells her, "but whoever drinks of the water that I shall give him will never thirst." Then his sense of the inexorable passage of time rises in him again, and "The hour is coming," he says, "when neither on this mountain nor in Jerusalem will you worship the Father." Then "The hour is coming and now is when the true worshippers will worship the Father in spirit and truth." The hour is so nearly at hand that in a sense it is at hand already: the hour of the Kingdom's coming when this insouciant lady and everyone else must make their fateful decisions for it or against it. Which way the lady herself finally decided, the Gospel of John never tells us, but the part of her conversation with Jesus that appears to have impressed her most was his strange ability to tell her about the five men she had married and the rather less formal relationship she had entered into with the one she was currently keeping house with. This is at least the burden of the report she carried back to the city when she left him. She had met this perfectly marvelous fortuneteller, she informed them, and then added almost as an afterthought that it was possible he might be the Messiah too. The chances seem to be that it is as a fortuneteller that he has interested her most, however, and that if she makes it to the Kingdom in the end, it will be less her own doing than the doing of the Holy One, who has a soft spot in his heart for high-stepping ladies in slippers with pointed toes.

Again and again as their accounts of Jesus' ministry unfold, the Gospels convey in spite of themselves that it was something less than the brilliant success that the extraordinary circumstances of his birth seemed to foreshadow. He tells parables that are simplicity itself, yet even the people closest to him often fail to understand them. He miraculously feeds a crowd of five thousand that comes to see him, but there is no record that he made a single convert. When he went back to Nazareth, his friends said, "He is beside himself," and there is reason to believe that his own mother and brothers were confused too.

On a number of occasions he chides the disciples for their lack of faith, those men who of all men had most reason to be faithful. When he pictured the end of the world and the coming of the Son of Man in his glory; and predicted that "this generation will not pass away till all these things come to pass," — all you can say is that, as things turned out, he was wrong.

And finally there was Lazarus, the friend from Bethany whom he loved and whose sisters he loved. When word was brought to him that Lazarus was ill, he said, "This illness is not unto death," and when on the contrary it killed him, Jesus was still able to speak words which his followers to this day treasure as among the most precious he ever spoke: "I am the resurrection and the life; he who believes in me, though he dies, yet shall he live, and whoever lives and believes in me shall never die." But when he went to Bethany and actually faced the sisters in their terrible grief, he could find for the moment no more such brave and hopeful words. "He was deeply moved in spirit," the evangelist writes, and then that shortest, bluntest verse in the entire New Testament: "Jesus wept."

If we could understand all that lay behind those tears, we would understand much about him, more maybe than it is well for us to understand; but to the degree that he

64. The Raising of Lazarus. *Oil on canvas. Karl Isakson. Sweden, contemporary.*

112

Jesus Turning Water into Wine

65. The Marriage at Cana. *Crayon on paper. Mary Hammatt, age 10. U.S.A., contemporary.*

was, whatever else, a human being like ourselves, we can understand at least something. It was presumably the naked fact itself that staggered him there in Bethany — death not as a distant darkness that his great faith was light enough to see him through; death not as a universal condition; but death as *this* death and darkness which he saw written across the swollen faces of the two women who stood there before him. Whatever Jesus may at other moments have seen as rising bright as hope beyond it, at

this particular moment death was a darkness he had no

heart to see beyond. Maybe it was more than that. "Could not he who opened the eyes of the blind have kept this man from dying?" some of the bystanders muttered in his hearing. It is hard not to believe that in the abyss of his being Jesus was asking himself the same dark question.

It is hard not to believe that it was himself as well as Lazarus that he wept for there. And that what he must have been tempted to see as the defeat and failure of everything that he had given his life to proclaim was, in some unspeakable measure, the failure and defeat even of his God. Even when he goes to the tomb and raises his old friend up, you feel that the death and the defeat of it are not entirely undone. Jesus stands there in his red robe (64) with one arm raised crying, "Lazarus come out!" but there is no look of triumph in his face or in the faces of the sisters who recoil behind him. What has appeared in the doorway of the stone tomb is a shrouded, black-faced ruin. It is not a living man who prepares to come out again into the unsparing light of day but a living corpse.

If death was to be truly defeated, it was only by dying himself that Jesus believed he could defeat it. If he was to reach the hearts of men, it was only by suffering his own heart to be broken on their behalf that he believed he could reach them. To heal the sick and restore sight to the blind; to preach good news to the poor and liberty to the captives; to wear himself out with his endless teaching and traveling the whole length and breadth of the land — it had not worked because it was not enough. There had to be more. "He set his face to go to Jerusalem," the Gospel says, and it was a journey from which he seems to have known that he would both never return and return always even unto the end of time and beyond. □

115

"Gentle Jesus... the merchant of dreams."

SADAO WATANABE 1970

IOANNES DE HEME
SEN ME FECIT
1573

LAST SUPPER

73. The Last Supper and the Washing of the Feet. *Tempera and gold leaf on parchment. From a psalter. French, probably Paris, about 1260.*

PRECEEDING PAGE

72. The Last Supper, *detail. Limestone relief. Germany, Lower Rhine, late 15th century.*

For every man there finally comes not just a last time but a whole calendar of last times — the last time he sees his child, his wife, his friend. The last time he takes a walk along the beach or sees the rain fall. The last time he makes love or writes a letter, builds a fire, hears his name spoken. It is part of the mercy of things that he rarely knows when each last time comes, is never sure when he is saying goodbye for good. Even the old man dying in his bed believes that he will feel the touch of a human hand again before he's done or hear the drawing of the blind, smell breakfast, drift off one more time into an old man's dozing. For some it is given to know — the criminal watching the sun come up on the morning of his execution, the suicide writing his note — but even for them there must always be the wild hope that somehow a miracle will happen to save them.

But for Jesus because he believed he had to die in order to save the world, there could be no hope for anything from the world to save him from dying. God was the power that he believed filled and sustained him, but it was God who had made him powerless. The miracle was to be that there would be no miracle. When it came time for him to eat his last meal with his friends, he knew it was his last. He was to be spared nothing.

For all their tendency to propagandize and prettify, the Gospels, at the same time, disarm us again and again with their helpless honesty. If there are certain events that they cannot tell without improving on them a little with each retelling — the birth, for instance — there are others that almost in spite of themselves they seem unable to tell except in the curt monosyllables of fact. There are the various blunderings of the disciples, for instance; or the crucifixion where even John resists the temptation to put a long farewell into the mouth of the crucified one; or the resurrection which takes place in confusion and half-light when everybody who should have been there is off somewhere else. And the same thing holds true in their accounts of this final meal that he lived to eat with his friends.

It would have been only human to picture it as an unusually successful affair with the disciples rising to the occasion as never before and Jesus presiding over them as the perfect host, serene and radiant and at peace to the last. But that is not the way the Gospels present it at all. True to form, the disciples start bickering about which of them is to be regarded as the greatest. In that very room where they had every reason to know that something fateful and tragic was about to happen to the leader they had sworn they loved, it is their own fate they are worried about as they set about jockeying for position. "Let the greatest among you become as the youngest and the leader as one who serves," Jesus says, and you can hear the weariness in his voice as he says it, wondering if it can be possible after all he has tried to show them both with his words and with his life that they have still missed the whole point of everything.

128   Peter is the one of them who shows some signs of under-

standing when he protests, "Lord, I am ready to go with you to prison and to death," but not even in him does Jesus see grounds for much hope. "Peter, the cock will not crow this day until you three times deny that you know me," he tells him, and you can hear the silence that settles over the table like a mist. Not only will Peter deny him, Jesus says, but one of them sitting there is going to betray him, and no sooner are the words out of his mouth than their recriminations begin. As a moment before, they wanted to know which of them was to be the hero of the piece, now they want to know which will be the villain. Nothing is more important to them than that the score be kept. It is to the disciple sitting nearest him, the disciple whom we are told he especially loved, that Jesus identifies the one he means. "It is he to whom I shall give this morsel when I have dipped it," he whispers, and the one who takes it from his hands and slips out into the night is Judas, the son of Simon Iscariot.

Jesus knows that it is their last supper together and he makes no secret of it. "This is my body," he says, picking up the bread. He breaks it in two and gives it away to them — "take . . . eat . . ." And then the wine. "This is my blood which is poured out," he tells them. "All of you drink it," and while the stain of it is still dark on their lips, he says, "I shall not drink again of this fruit of the vine until that day when I drink it new with you in my Father's house."

The great Messianic Feast to take place beyond time — there was this single, soul-restoring dream that even he must have had a hard time dreaming in that stuffy room full of frightened Jews. But he makes it clear that in the

meantime there will be little enough to restore their souls.

When he first sent them out as disciples, he reminds them, he told them to take no purse or bag or sandals, nothing to arm themselves with against the world, "but now let him who has a purse take it and likewise a bag, and let him who has no sword sell his mantle and buy one." This side of Paradise there is to be no Paradise, and this side of the peace which passeth all understanding there is to be no peace that they are likely to understand. They are going to have to fight fire with fire, he tells these feckless men, and if it is to be a fire that lights the way to truth, it will also kindle the blaze of their own cruel martyrdom. He promises them no less.

And then they sing a hymn, the Gospels say. Their mouths spit-dry, not one of them with heart enough to carry a tune, their voices thin and quavering as they try to keep their spirits up. They belt out some crazy, holy song and leave for the Mount of Olives where Jesus says, "You will all fall away."

Whatever else it was not, it was at least human, this final feast. One hardly knows whether to laugh or to weep. They were no better and no worse than they had always been, the twelve feasters. They were themselves to the end. And if there is a kind of black comedy about them, the way the Gospels paint the scene, there is a kind of battered courage about them too. Even though they knew what was coming, knew even what their own unedifying part in it was to be, they stuck to their guns, all but one of them. And in the long run, if not the short, they stuck to their Jesus too. God makes his saints out of fools and sinners because there is nothing much else to make them of. God makes his Messiah out of a fierce and fiercely gentle man who spills himself out, his very flesh and blood, as though

74. The Last Supper. *Limestone relief. Germany, Lower Rhine, late 15th century.*

130

it is only a loaf of bread and a cup of sweet red wine that he is spilling.

Maybe stone is the best medium for representing their last supper. Stone is intractable, solid, stark. It is something that you can get your hands on and pit your weight against, something that does not lend itself to too great subtlety or sweetness. The crude honesty of stone, no matter how artfully worked, never deceives the eye as paint on canvas can into taking it for anything but what it is, never lets you quite forget that sore muscles and sweat and smashed fingers went into the working.

Jesus sits at a circular table in a relief sculpted out of limestone by a fifteenth century German (74). He is surrounded by his twelve friends, and because of the way the relief is done on a flat plane, it is as if we are looking down at them from a considerable height or as if they are receding from us through space and time. The sculptor has not posed them but caught them unawares with their hands frozen in the middle of gestures, their faces unguarded and lost between expressions. One old man stares up at the ceiling with a look of tipsy bravado, and another with a great hooked nose and a cap with earflaps shakes his fist at a friend across from him who seems to have his mind elsewhere, as to a degree all of them do. They are all old men, and hardly a one of them is paying any attention to Jesus. Their eyes are open, but there is something oddly sightless about them so that even the one or two who are looking at him do not seem to see him. The beloved disciple has fallen asleep with his chin resting on the table. Jesus has his right hand resting lightly on the man's forehead.

Jesus is also an old man. His hair has receded, and there

are deep creases at the corners of his hooded eyes. His head is tilted slightly to one side. The dark shadow of his lips suggests the shadow of a smile or maybe he is starting to say something. His right hand seems to have been broken off at the wrist, but perhaps it held a cup once, and he is about to say, "This is my blood." Perhaps it held a bit of bread and he is about to identify Judas by handing it to him. It is possible that Judas may be the one looking up at the ceiling and only pretending to be tipsy and brave as maybe the beloved disciple is only pretending to be asleep. In any case, it is Jesus who dominates the scene.

The sculptor has given him no halo or any other badge of honor to single him out, but somehow he has managed to suggest that Jesus is more fully present at that stone table than any of the rest of them. The disciples all have the air of men lost in their own thoughts, but Jesus belongs totally to this time, this place. His gaze begins to move slowly from face to face around the table — those great heavy-lidded eyes that have seen everything, the bearded mouth, the porous stone cheeks with pools of darkness in them. You can see in his face both how it was that the old men had had no choice but to follow when he first called them to him and how it is that they cannot bring themselves to look directly at him now. There is a dream-like quality about the scene as the fifteenth century German carves it, but it is a stone dream, a dream which hangs heavy in the memory long after waking, that cries out to be understood and at the same time — unyielding and impenetrable as Stonehenge — defies understanding.

There is the Last Supper also as madness and hallucination. Jesus is a madman (75). He sits cringing at a small café table covered with a white cloth. With one hand he

134

is clutching a loaf of bread to him as though his life depends on it, as though there is nothing anywhere in the known universe that does not depend on it. He has his other hand cupped above it to swat away flies or demons if it should come to that. The only other person at the table with him is the beloved disciple, who is a plump child with yellow curls. The child is leaning forward with his bare elbows on the table and his hands clasped at his chin, his gaze heavenward, in a parody of pious exaltation. Another child or a dwarf kneels out of Jesus' sight in front of the table. It carries a thorn twig behind its back and is reaching up to the edge of the table-top with one clenched fist. A vague, white figure stands near Jesus staring down at the loaf of bread and clapping its hands. A giant with a pinhead teeters on bare feet, praying.

Jesus is a paranoid. He believes he is God and that the world is out to get him. The only ones he can bear near him are children. A bird is hovering over the head of the child at his side, but Jesus knows that it is the Holy Ghost in diabolically clever disguise, the Paraclete as parakeet. He also knows about the cruel thorn the dwarf is hiding. But he is not letting on that he knows. Though he pretends not to notice the shadowy figure clapping its hands, it is from the possibility of its touch that he is cringing. A ragged flower withering behind him betrays what is in the air. There is something floating in the glass of wine, and he has left it untouched. With his shoulders hunched and lopsided, he is humming a casual little tune as he gazes up at some spot on the ceiling. No one would ever guess from his vacant expression that he is ready to strangle with his own bare hands anyone who tries to take his precious loaf away. It is his body, his soul's

75. The Last Supper. *Oil on canvas. Ernst Josephson. Sweden, contemporary.*

darling, and as he slyly pulls it a little closer to him across the white cloth, an explosion goes off inside his head like Hiroshima. Fragments of fire shoot out of him like sky-rockets. Centuries may pass before it is possible to assess the full extent of the disaster. If Jesus was not the Messiah, then he was a lunatic who thought he was. It is difficult to see how there can be any middle ground.

In his own way, Paul would have perhaps understood this painting too, Paul as the only one who ever dared speak of the foolishness of God, of the crucifixion itself as folly, of the folly of his own preaching. If the world is sane, then Jesus is mad as a hatter and the Last Supper is the Mad Tea Party. The world says, Mind your own business, and Jesus says, There is no such thing as your own business. The world says, Follow the wisest course and be a success, and Jesus says, Follow me and be cruci-fied. The world says, Drive carefully — the life you save may be your own — and Jesus says, Whoever would save his life will lose it, and whoever loses his life for my sake will find it. The world says, Law and order, and Jesus says, Love. The world says, Get and Jesus says, Give. In terms of the world's sanity, Jesus is crazy as a coot, and any-body who thinks he can follow him without being a little crazy too is laboring less under a cross than under a delusion.

"We are fools for Christ's sake," Paul says, faith says — the faith that ultimately the foolishness of God is wiser than the wisdom of men, the lunacy of Jesus saner than the grim sanity of the world. Through the eyes of faith too, the Last Supper, though on one level a tragic farewell and failure, perhaps farce, is also, at its deepest

136 level, the foreshadowing of great hope and the bodying

Jesus at the Last Supper

76. The Last Supper. *Crayon on paper. Angel Baudoin, age 10. U.S.A., contemporary.*

forth of deep mystery. Frail, fallible, foolish as he knows the disciples to be, Jesus feeds them with himself. The bread is his flesh, the wine his blood, and they are all of them including Judas to eat and drink him down. They are to take his life into themselves and come alive with it, to be his hands and feet in a world where he no longer has hands and feet, to feed his lambs. "Do this in remembrance of me," Paul quotes him as saying. In eating the bread and drinking the wine, they are to remember him, Jesus tells

137 them, and to remember him not merely in the sense of

77. The Last Supper. *Oil on canvas. Bernard Buffet. France, 1961.*

letting their minds drift back to him in the dim past but in the sense of recalling him to the immediate present. They are to remember him the way when we remember someone we love who has died, he is alive again within us to the point where we can all but hear him speak and our hearts kindle to the reality of his presence.

In its fullest sense, remembering is far more than the long backward glance of nostalgia, and in its fullest sense the symbol of bread and wine is far more than symbol. It

138 is part of the mystery of any symbol always to contain

something of the power of the thing symbolized just as it is more than a mere piece of painted cloth that makes your pulse quicken when you come upon your country's flag in a foreign land, more than a mere sound that gladdens your spirit when you hear someone speak the name of an absent friend. When in remembrance of Jesus, the disciples ate the bread and drank the wine, it was more than mere bread and wine they were dealing with, and for all the tragic and ludicrous battles Christians have fought with each other for centuries over what actually takes place at the Mass, the Eucharist, Communion, or whatever they call it, they would all seem to agree that something extraordinary takes place. Even if the priest is a fraud, the bread a tasteless wafer, the wine not wine at all but temperance grapejuice, the one who comes to this outlandish meal in faith may find there something to feed his deepest hunger, may feel stirring within himself a life even more precious, more urgent, more near than his own.

Or of course he may find nothing. Unlike magic whereby if you say abracadabra right the spell will always work, religion does not make anything always work; and faith cannot be sure of things happening the way it wants, because it is God who makes things happen the way he wants — faith can only wait in hope and trust. Sometimes God makes himself known by his presence, sometimes by his absence, and for both faith and unfaith the absence of God is dark and menacing.

Bernard Buffet paints a Last Supper (77) where God is absent, where it is not life that is distributed to the faithful but death. The head of Jesus is a skull, the nose and mouth fleshless, the downcast eyes two empty slits. A lightless halo bristles like quills out of his bare scalp. He is sur-

78. Christ and St. John from the Last Supper. *Painted on silk. China, 19th-20th century.*

rounded on the far side of the table by eleven of the disciples. Like him they are dressed in robes of the same livid purple as the wine which stands in three glass decanters in front of them. Like him they are living corpses, their faces as white as the cloth the table is laid with, their expressions all variations on the single theme of despair. The only suggestion of movement among them is in their eyes. They are all, like Jesus, studiously looking away from the only thing there is to look at, which is Judas.

Judas is in front of the table with his back to them. He

140

is hurrying away to do what he has been appointed to do, but there is nothing furtive about the way he does it. His jaw is clenched and resolute, and of all of them he is the only one who seems to be looking not away from something but toward something. Of all of them, his is the only face which, though dead like theirs, has some echo of life in it. He knows where he is going, and he is hastening to go there. There is the remnant of something almost like pity in his look. One has the feeling that it is out of something almost like pity for the living dead behind him that he is hurrying forth now to arrange a death for them that will be complete and final. If there is any salvation in a world where God is absent, it can only be in oblivion. If there is any savior at this table, it is Judas.

Buffet's Judas is the only one of the twelve who does not wear a halo perhaps because he is the only one of them who knows that there is no such thing, but in a Chinese painting on silk (78) he wears one no less bright than the other disciples. One assumes that it is a measure of the infinite tact of Jesus not to have deprived him of it. In a dove gray kimono with a moonstone at his forehead, Jesus is about to hand him the ricecake that will mark him as a traitor, but he does it with such exquisite graciousness that it becomes part of a ceremonial. He holds the wafer between his thumb and forefinger with the other fingers arched beautifully back, and he is looking at Judas with a courteous smile faint on his lips. A branch of bamboo is visible through the large, circular window. A paper lantern above the table casts a luminous circle on the wall behind Jesus. Most of the disciples have discreetly withdrawn, and their red lacquer stools stand empty, their porcelain bowls and chopsticks as yet untouched.

FOLLOWING PAGES

79. The Last Supper, *detail. Oil on canvas. Bernard Buffet. France, 1961.*

80. The Last Supper, *detail. Painted on silk. China, 19th-20th century.*

141

The beloved disciple is feigning sleep rather than behold his colleague's disgrace; the only other disciple present sits gazing down at his fingertips which he has brought together in front of him so that they just touch.

Judas has sunk to one knee on the tiled floor and reaches out beseechingly toward his master. One is reminded of the tale of the Chinese emperor who was obliged by reasons of state to have one of his friends decapitated. To make it as painless as possible, on the day appointed for the execution the Emperor arranged for his friend a great round of entertainment to distract him from the melancholy business at hand. Fireworks shot into the sky and fountains played. There were tumblers and dancing girls and magicians. Finally, unable to bear the suspense any longer, the condemned man came to the Emperor and thanking him for his superb generosity in providing such a spectacle nevertheless begged him to let his decapitation take place immediately. "Ah, but my dear friend," the Emperor said, "it has already taken place."

"What you are going to do," Jesus says, "do quickly."

What Judas is going to do, he does in a garden, but though he goes about it as quickly as he can, there is a little time to wait before he gets there. It is night, and they are all tired. Jesus tells them, "My soul is very sorrowful, even to death," and then asks the disciples to stay and watch for him while he goes off to pray. One thinks of the stirring and noble way others have met their deaths — the equanimity of Socrates as he raised the hemlock to his lips, the exaltation of Joan as they bound her to the stake, Nathan Hale's "I only regret that I have but one life to lose for my country." Jesus sounds like none of

them. Maybe it is because it is to the ones who are most

81. The Agony in the Garden *and* The Kiss of Judas. *Tempera and gold leaf on parchment. From a psalter. French, probably Paris, about 1260.*

fully alive that death comes most unbearably. His prayer is, "Abba, Father, all things are possible for thee; remove this cup from me; yet not what I will but what thou wilt," this tormented muddle of a prayer which Luke says made him sweat until it "became like great drops of blood falling down upon the ground." He went back to find some solace in the company of his friends then, but he found them all asleep when he got there. "The spirit indeed is willing, but the flesh is weak," he said, and you feel that it was to himself that he was saying it as well as to them.

A French monk has illuminated the event with tempera and gold leaf on the parchment page of a Psalter (81). Jesus kneels in the garden with his prayer falling out of his mouth like a scroll while a little distance behind him the disciples have dozed off with their heads in their hands. From the expression on their faces, you can tell that they are having good dreams. You can imagine Jesus hesitating a moment before he waked them to the havoc that the monk has painted just below on the page: the temple guards chinking across the grass in their crusaders' mail and one of the disciples cutting off the ear of the high priest's slave with his sword. Matthew has Jesus chide the disciple for his brashness, and Luke, going one step further, has him touch the ear and heal it, but Mark, writing earliest, gives no indication that Jesus had time even to notice.

All three of them, however, agree about Judas. It was Judas who led the authorities to the garden a little way east of Jerusalem, and it was Judas who signaled to them which of the men standing there in the dark was Jesus. The way he signaled, of course, was by going up to him and kissing him, and when Dante came to write his *In-*

82. The Kiss of Judas. *Oakwood relief. Germany, Lower Rhine, early 16th century.*

146

ferno, it was because of this kiss that he placed Judas in the nethermost circle of hell, his torment being to spend eternity in the icy Lake of Cocytus while Satan, winged like a bat, gnaws at his frozen flesh.

Already in this sculpture of polished oak (82) Judas seems frozen at least in time as he leans forward with one hand on Jesus' chest, their beards just touching. There is something tentative in the way he goes about it as if for a moment he is not sure that he has found the right man or that, having found him, he can remember what his kiss is supposed to signal. We cannot see his face very well, just a part of his profile — the lines on his forehead and at the corner of one eye, the curve of his cheek. It is easier to condemn a man to the nethermost circle of hell when you cannot see such things too clearly.

Jesus' eyes are closed, and he seems to be unsteady on his feet, leaning a little backward and clutching on to his robe. The sculptor was German, but there is something Slavic about the face with its high cheekbones and faintly slanted eyes. He could be Dostoevski's Father Zossima, who said, "Fathers and teachers, I ponder, 'What is hell?' I maintain that hell is the suffering of being unable to love." He has his left hand raised in benediction.

The soldiers are there with their swords and lanterns. The high priest's slave is whimpering over his wounded ear. There can be no doubt in Jesus' mind what the kiss of Judas means, but it is Judas that he is blessing, and Judas that he is prepared to go out and die for now. Judas is only the first in a procession of betrayers two thousand years long. If Jesus were to exclude him from his love and forgiveness, to one degree or another he would have to exclude mankind.

148

*"This
is my body...
This
is my blood."*

Maybe this is all in the mind of Jesus as he stands there with his eyes closed, or possibly there is nothing in his mind at all. As he feels his friend's lips graze his check, for an instant maybe he feels nothing else. It is another of his last times. On this last evening of his life he has eaten his last meal, and this is the last time that he will ever feel the touch of another human being except in torment. It is not the Lamb of God and his butcher who meet here, but two old friends embracing in a garden because they both of them know that they will never see one another again.

☐

83. The Agony in the Garden. *Tempera and oil on panel. Predella from an altarpiece. Raphael Sanzio. Italy, early 16th century.*

FOLLOWING PAGES

84. The Last Supper. *Bronze cast plaquette. Dmitri Ferentinos. Greece, Athens, about 1960.*

85. The Last Supper, *detail. Oil on canvas. Salvador Dali. Spanish, 1955.*

86. The Agony in the Garden. *Fresco. Giovanni Canavesio. France, La Brigue, about 1492.*

9389

CRUCIFIXION

PRECEEDING PAGE

87. Crucifixion. *Champlevé enamel. France, Limoges, about 1200.*

88. Crucifixion. *Ivory. African.*

158

By the late Middle Ages, Christian piety had evolved a detailed tradition about what happened to Jesus on his way from the trial before Pilate, the Roman procurator, to the site of his execution and finally his grave. The Stations of the Cross as they have come to be known represent the various incidents along that somber route: Jesus sentenced to death, receiving his cross, stumbling three times under the weight of it and then a passer-by compelled to shoulder it the rest of the way for him; Jesus meeting his mother, meeting a woman named Veronica, who wiped his face with her veil which ever afterwards bore the bloody imprint of his face upon it, addressing the women of Jerusalem with "Do not weep for me but weep for yourselves and your children;" Jesus stripped of his garments, nailed to the cross, dying, laid in his tomb. There are fourteen of them all-told, and they are sometimes found carved or painted around the walls of churches so that especially during Lent and Passiontide the devout can move from one to another in meditation and prayer. Some of the incidents are entirely legendary—the meetings with Veronica and Mary, for instance—and some are to be found in the New Testament although by and large there are few such details about the road to Golgotha there. But there is of course nothing that occurred during those last few hours of Jesus' life, and nothing that the mind of faith can imagine having occurred, that has not been the subject of endless conjecture and innumerable works of art.

Before sending him off to his crucifixion, Pilate had Jesus scourged. It was a not uncommon practice at the time, especially in the case of criminals who were not Roman citizens. The Greek word found in the Gospels for *scourge* suggests that what was used may have been the *flagra*, which were iron chains ending in little metal balls or cords knotted over small bones at the ends, or it may have been a knout made of leather thongs, the *horribile flagellum* that Horace refers to in his *Satires*. In either case it was not unusual for the criminal to die under this preliminary punishment, thus being spared the greater one to follow. Jesus was not so fortunate.

Many artists have been unable to resist exploiting the horror of this scene, and the museums and churches of the world teem with Grand Guignol Christs with their flesh torn and bleeding as Pilate's guards lay on with a will. For some of the painters and sculptors, it was undoubtedly a chance to cater to the sadist in all men including themselves, the fascination with torture and pain and death here given religious sanction. But they undoubtedly had other motives too, among them the fascination with the idea that what writhed beneath the lash was not just a man but the God-man, the man in whose flesh God himself walked among us and suffered not just at the hands of sinful men but at the same time for their sakes.

Part of what it means to be a man is to know as all men must the misery and affront of physical pain. In the case of the crucifixion, even the most gruesome represen-

89. Christ of the Flagellation. *Oil on canvas. David Alfaro Siqueiros. Mexico, 20th century.*

160

tations convey a sense that the agony of Jesus on the cross was in some measure transcended by his knowledge of what he was achieving through it, or at least the viewer brings that sense to these crucifixions. But in the case of the scourging, there seems to be only the unadorned agony itself, the tortured flesh with no dream of divine mission to assuage it.

This is what primarily confronts us in a contemporary oil (89) that shows Jesus bound to the whipping post facing us but with his head wrenched sideways in an ecstasy of pain as the lashes fall. In bullfighting, a *veronica* is that dangerous maneuver when without moving from his place the matador slowly swings his cape away from the charging bull, and Jesus here is a huge bull of a man, bearded, with a broken nose and blood trickling down his temples from a barbed-wire crown. His manacled hands are thrust forward at us, the knuckles abraded and raw.

A wooden Christ from fifteenth century Spain (90) speaks much this same word to us — the naked flesh is lacerated with crimson drops falling from brow to groin like a mantilla — but here another word is spoken too. The scourging has stopped, and Jesus stands with his

90. The Man of Sorrows. *Wood polychromed. Austria, Styria, 15th century.*

hands crossed on his breast and the scourge tucked under one arm like a scepter. His eyes are still heavy with suffering under the circlet of thorns, but their expression is human again or more than human, not wild and animal-like that baited bull of a man with the ruined hands.

On the twelfth century bronze doors of Saint Zeno's in Verona (91), the expression on Jesus' face has become more than anything else superbly scornful. There is something hopelessly ineffectual about his tormentors in their coolie hats and long skirts, and he knows it. One of them is

163

91. The Flagellation. *Bronze relief. Church doors at San Zeno, Verona. Italy, early 12th century.*

scratching his cheek in doltish confusion, another pulls at his beard as though uncertain what to do next. The man who is doing the lashing wields the scourge like a peacock fan. Here the pain is no longer the pain of Jesus as much as it is the befuddled pain of his tormentors as it begins to dawn on them, in bronze, that what they are in the process of destroying is just possibly themselves.

The sentence passed, the scourging done, Jesus is given the cross to carry on his own shoulders to the hill of his execution like Hitler's Jews being forced to dig their own

164

92. Christ Carrying the Cross. *Embroidered chasuble. Brussels, 16th century.*

common grave before the bullets mowed them down at the lip of it. This "station" has been caught in silk on an embroidered English chasuble, the sleeveless vestment worn by a priest at the celebration of the Mass. Jesus is bent nearly double under the weight, and his eyes are glazed and staring with the look of plaintive exhaustion of a man set a test of strength that he knows he will fail. The great load rests mainly on his shoulders, and his right arm is draped limply over the vertical shaft. One soldier

165 seems to be trying to help him to his feet from behind

93. Christ with Thorns. *Felt banner. Norman LaLiberté. U.S.A. contemporary.*

while two others have their arms raised to bludgeon him forward. A fourth holds a trumpet to his silken lips, and all about them the air is stitched with gold as the procession starts to mount the Via Dolorosa of a fifteenth century priest's gorgeousness.

Weakened almost beyond endurance by the ordeal of the scourge, Jesus is unable to carry his burden very far, "and they seized one Simon of Cyrene, who was coming in from the country, and laid on him the cross, to carry it behind Jesus," Luke writes in his Gospel. Thus it is an in-

166

nocent bystander who becomes the first to take up his cross and follow him albeit not voluntarily, we are told, and having other plans altogether as he came in from the country on some errand long since lost in history. Centuries of Christian sermonizing have depicted him as symbolic of the true disciple taking up his cross as the Lord commanded, but one cannot help suspecting that like Lincoln's joke about the man being ridden out of town on a rail, if it hadn't been for the honor of the thing, he would have just as soon walked.

Cyrene was a town on the northern coast of Africa opposite Crete, and some have held that Simon was a black. There would be some good sermons in that too. But no one has woven a more glittering cloak of pious fancies around poor, hapless Simon than the second century Gnostics as mentioned by Irenaeus. Convinced that Jesus was a purely spiritual being whose human body was only an illusion, and horrified by the claim that he had actually suffered material pain at Calvary, the Gnostics held that as soon as Simon shouldered the cross, Jesus magically transformed the man into his own likeness so that it was Simon who was crucified when the time came while Jesus stood on the sidelines mocking the executioners. Gnosticism as such has long been out of fashion, but there are echoes of it still among those who in excessive veneration of the godness of Jesus shy away from his man-ness, from the fact that like the rest of us he did not just have a body but *was* a body, a body that he might never have been able to drag another step farther if Simon of Cyrene had not been strong-armed into shouldering the cross for him.

You see something of the same gnostic tendency at work in the bloodless, ghostly imprint of Jesus' face on

167

Veronica's veil (94). There is something stylized, almost stagey about it — the brow furrowed, the lips parted in a sigh of exhaustion and grief but the features classically handsome and unmarred. It looks like a tragic mask which the great actor wore while the play called for it but underneath which he continued to be always the serene master of his art. This same impression is even more vividly conveyed by a sixteenth century oak carving (95) where the face of Jesus is rendered more masklike still by being not painted on the veil but carved into it with empty eyes through which you can imagine the divine masker peering. It is not hard to sympathize with the Gnostics in their heresy. There is something in every man that wants his god, if he has one, to be utterly transcendent and holy, utterly unstained by history and beyond the reach of all the suffering that is fitting for the creation but beneath the dignity of the creator. If God is to save us from the raging torrent of our tragic and sinful existence, he must himself stand safely on the bank lest he be caught up and swept away with the rest of us.

Christian orthodoxy feels this as well as gnostic heterodoxy, and it is out of something like the same impulse that Paul writes of "the glory of God in the face of Christ." But never squeamish about paradox, Christian orthodoxy sees the glory of man in that face too, and the glory of this man was to leap into the torrent with sinners, struggling against the same terrible odds and determined to save them from drowning even if it cost him his life.

One remembers again the Suffering Servant of Isaiah whom Jesus himself remembered and whose face is described as "marred beyond human semblance, and his form beyond that of the sons of men . . . he had no form

96. St. Veronica. *Oil on canvas. Bernard Buffet. France, 1961.*

or comeliness that we should look at him and no beauty that we should desire him.'' For Jesus, as the Suffering Servant, the Divine Actor, was so caught up in his holy part that the two became inseparable, and the gnostic Christ who only masqueraded as a man of sorrows becomes the Jesus of the classic creeds who was as fully human as he was fully divine so that when Veronica wiped his bloody face with her veil, it was a real man's face that left its stamp upon it.

171   It is the grotesque parody of such a face that Bernard

Buffet paints on his version of the veil (96), a face so ghoulishly caricatured that we recoil from it as from an open sore — that clotted hair, those lips shrunken back to reveal the dry, white teeth of a dead animal. Buffet's Veronica wears a look of disgust as she holds the thing up by her fingertips like a soiled sheet. It is the scandal of the incarnation that she holds, the shame of a god who has so wallowed in the muck and misery of the world that he has become indistinguishable from it. Veronica and her ladies seem to be telling us that a god who would so demean himself cannot really be God, and it is beneath the dignity of man to worship him.

It is some anonymous African craftsman carving a face only a few inches high (97) who tells us that a god who would so demean himself, if there is such a god, is the only god worth living and dying for. It is the face of Christ crowned with thorns, a black Christ carved on a book end out of some dark wood that has been sanded and mellowed to a soft sheen. You ache to run your fingers down the bridge of the nose and the great, full lips; to trace the cool plane of the cheeks where the swirl of the grain has become the track of dried tears, the scar running down into one eyebrow where the wood has cracked. There is no way of saying all that shines out of such a face other than the way the wood has said it. Compassion, beauty, sorrow, majesty, love — as words they are so freighted with meaning that they finally founder. The wood is mute. What it tells us is simply all there is to tell about what it means to be black, what it means to be a man, what it means to be God.

Finally the crucifixion itself. It was a Roman punishment, not a Jewish one, and whatever the connivance of

97. Christ with the Crown of Thorns. *Wood. Africa, 20th century.*

172

98. Christ Nailed to the Cross. *Fresco.
Giovanni Canavesio. France, La Brigue,
about 1492.*

the Jews may have been, it was the Romans who sentenced
him to it and carried it out. It was a punishment for slaves
and considered an outrage if inflicted on a Roman citizen.
Usually the cross was not very high and constructed in the
shape of a T. The condemned man was hoisted on to it
with his hands nailed or tied to the crossbar and his feet
to the upright. Since the weight would have quickly torn
through the hands, the body was supported by a peg between the thighs or possibly some kind of support beneath
174 the feet. Death was usually a long time coming. Cramps

99. Crucifixion. *Oil on canvas. Bernard Buffet. France, 1970.*

started in the muscles of the forearms and then spread into the whole upper body, the abdomen, the legs. With this enormous burden on the heart, the pulse was inevitably slowed and the blood carried less and less oxygen to the lungs so that the victim slowly suffocated. Poisoned by waste matter that the heart was no longer strong enough to eliminate, the muscles were affected by spasms that caused excruciating pain. The ordeal often lasted as long as two or three days before the criminal finally ran out of strength and breath and died. Jesus was fortunate in

175

100. Corpus Christi. *Bronze gilt. France, Limoges, about 1240.*

lasting only a few hours.

"God so loved the world," John writes, "that he gave his only son, that whoever believes in him should not perish but have eternal life." That is to say that God so loved the world that he gave his only son even to this obscene horror; so loved the world that in some ultimately indescribable way and at some ultimately immeasurable cost he gave the world himself. Out of this terrible death, John says, came eternal life not just in the sense of resurrection to life after death but in the sense of life so precious

101. Crucifixion. *Wood. New Irlanda, Melanesia, 20th century.*

even this side of death that to live it is to stand with one foot already in eternity. To participate in the sacrificial life and death of Jesus Christ is to live already in his kingdom. This is the essence of the Christian message, the heart of the Good News, and it is why the cross has become the chief Christian symbol. A cross of all things—a guillotine, a gallows — but the cross at the same time as the crossroads of eternity and time, as the place where such a mighty heart was broken that the healing power of God himself could flow through it into a sick and broken world.

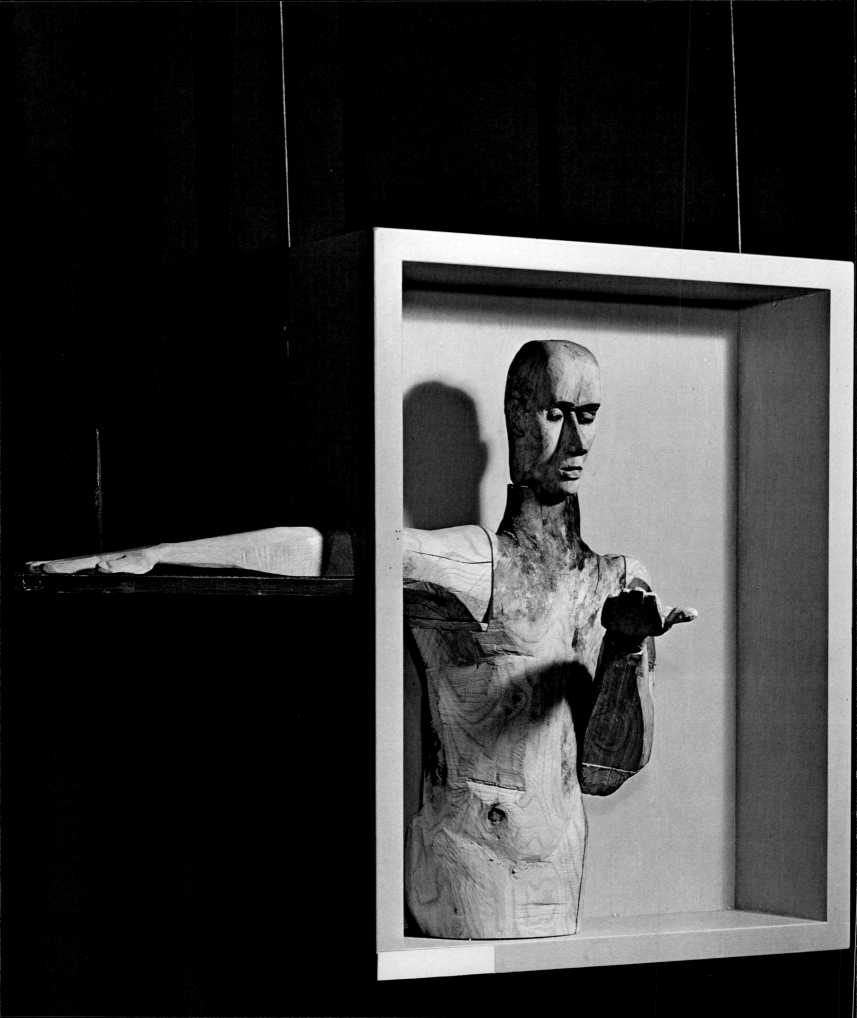

It was for this reason that of all the possible words they could have used to describe the day of his death, the word they settled on was "good." *Good* Friday.

The man on the cross was a man of flesh, but he was also the WORD made flesh, as John writes it in the great prologue to his Gospel, the Word that "became flesh and dwelt among us full of grace and truth." The Creator himself comes to dwell within his own creation, the Eternal within the temporal, the Invulnerable within the wound. It is as if Shakespeare could somehow have entered the world of *Hamlet*, say, the dramatist descending from the infinite dimensions of reality into the comparative dimensionlessness of his own drama, becoming a character in his own plot although he well knows its tragic denouement and submitting himself to all its limitations so that he can burst them asunder when the time comes and lead a tremendous *exeunt* by which his whole *dramatis personae* will become true persons at last.

Something like this is what seems to be suggested by a curious modern sculpture (102) which shows a wooden Jesus partially framed in a wooden rectangle. He has one

102. *"Ordet". Wood polychromed. Torsten Renqvist. Sweden, 1971.*

arm stretched out horizontally through the frame into darkness, the hand pierced by a long vertical nail. This impaled, projecting hand is the outerness of it, the drama of it and the pain. Within the frame is the innerness of it, the true heart of the dramatist which is both in the pain and beyond it. The face of Jesus is stern as death but alive and at peace. He is contemplating the palm of the other hand as though reading in it the play within the play, the destiny of destiny itself.

The outer pain, the inner peace — in depicting the crucifixion the artists tend always to emphasize one at the

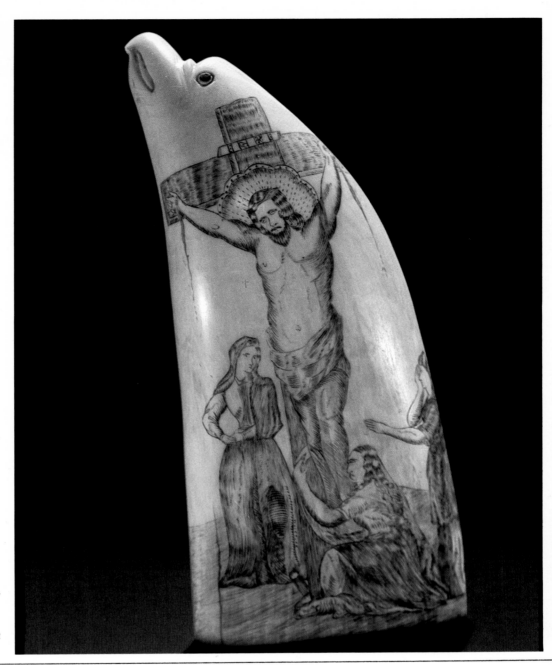

103. Crucifixion. *Bronze. Floriano Bodini. Italy, 1933.*

104. Crucifixion. *Scrimshaw. U.S.A., 19th century.*

expense of the other. Only the greatest of them manage somehow to do justice to them both.

Nowhere is the pain portrayed more staggeringly than in a twentieth century bronze by Floriano Bodini (103). Jesus is pitched forward from his cross, bent double at the waist like a pinned insect. He is kept from falling to the ground by two heavy spikes driven through his hands with their fingers clawing at the air. His arms are wrenched almost out of their sockets, his rib cage distended as he labors for breath. He is all skin and bones, knock-kneed

181

with agony. The bronze of his flesh is laid on like mud with a trowel. Some scrap of clothing flaps down from his naked hips, the skin of his face stretched tight as a mummy's over the skull. His cavernous mouth is wide open, the tongue swollen inside. He is retching out his life like vomit.

Some nineteenth century sailor (104) does him in scrimshaw, scratching him out with a knife on the tooth of a whale with its cusp whittled to look like a bird of prey. Here Jesus is shapeless and white, a barrel-chested Moby Dick of a man who seems to be melting like wax. Did the sailorman know the twenty-second Psalm that Jesus quoted from the cross with its "my heart is like wax, it is melted within my breast"? His spindly legs are almost gone, and one of the women who hover around him has circled them with her beefy, sailor-wife arms. What little is left of his hands is also going fast. The blood runs down from them like tallow.

On a medieval crucifix (105) his ivory flesh has gone brown like an old meerschaum, and he is glistening and slippery with dying. His hands and feet are clumsy and too big for him. His hair and beard are roped with sweat. A great, sad nose juts out over his pinched lips. His eyes look swollen shut. "Kings shall shut their mouths at him," Isaiah wrote of the Suffering Servant, meaning perhaps that kings clapped their hands to their mouths to stifle their cries of revulsion at the sight of him hanging there in that cloth of enamel and gold that somebody knotted around his waist as if to make it up to him for looking so unkingly in his passion, so shrunken and ugly and foolish for a king.

From a twelfth century crucifix (106) the cross has been lost, and all that remains is the body. With his arms

105. Crucifixion. *Ivory on bronze gilt and enamel. Spain, north, late 12th century.*

winged out wide and his head bent, Jesus is flying through the royal purple night. For the first time he looks definitely Semitic with the shape of his nose, the cut of his beard, the way he has somehow shrugged off his cross. He is Abraham, Shylock, Dreyfus, the Baal Shem. He is a Jew here, all Jews.

"You shall be to me a kingdom of priests and a holy nation," God told Moses on Mount Sinai. "These are the words you shall speak to the children of Israel." Right from the beginning the trouble was that Israel had no taste for being a kingdom of priests but chose rather to be a nation like any other nation, a power among powers. Israel's whole tragic history can be read as an attempt to escape its holy calling and the terrible price exacted of it for doing so. Again and again it tried by playing international politics to make its weight felt in history only to be again and again decimated by history. The northern kingdom fell to Assyria in the eighth century B.C., and in the sixth the Babylonians laid waste to Jerusalem in the south, burning Solomon's Temple and carrying the leaders off into captivity. For two hundred years afterwards the Persians held sway until in the fourth century Alexander the Great conquered Darius; and Israel became part of his empire, first under the Ptolomies, then under the Seleucids. After a brief period of independence, a civil war broke out between the two contending priest-kings, and when one of them called on Rome to intervene in his behalf, Pompey marched into Jerusalem with the Roman eagles, captured the second temple, massacred some twelve thousand Jews, and made all Palestine a tributary of Rome.

Throughout all these centuries there were always the prophets thundering out at king and people to remember

106. Corpus Christi. *Bronze gilt. France, about 1130.*

107. Crucifixion. *Ink and watercolor. W. C. Mirico. Italo-American, 20th century.*

their ancient mission to be the kingdom of priests that God had called them to be, but each time the prophetic cry went largely unheeded, and each time Israel went down to another defeat with only a remnant of the pious left to be, as Isaiah put it, a green branch growing out of a hewn stump. Remnant led to remnant until finally, in terms of New Testament faith, the remnant became just Jesus and his twelve disciples. When the last of the disciples abandoned him, the remnant became just Jesus himself.

186   The kingdom of priests was reduced at last to this One,

108. Crucifixion. *Oil on canvas. Spain, 17th century.*

who was both priest and sacrifice, and so it is Israel itself that hangs there on the cross, the suffering one who was "bruised for our iniquities and upon whom was the chastisement that made us whole." Jesus is all Jews and in a sense also the only Jew as he hovers there in the purple sky. It is out of his passion that the Church will be born as the new Israel, a kingdom of priests at last. It is through his intercession that at the end of history the holy city, New Jerusalem, will come down out of heaven like a bride

adorned for her husband.

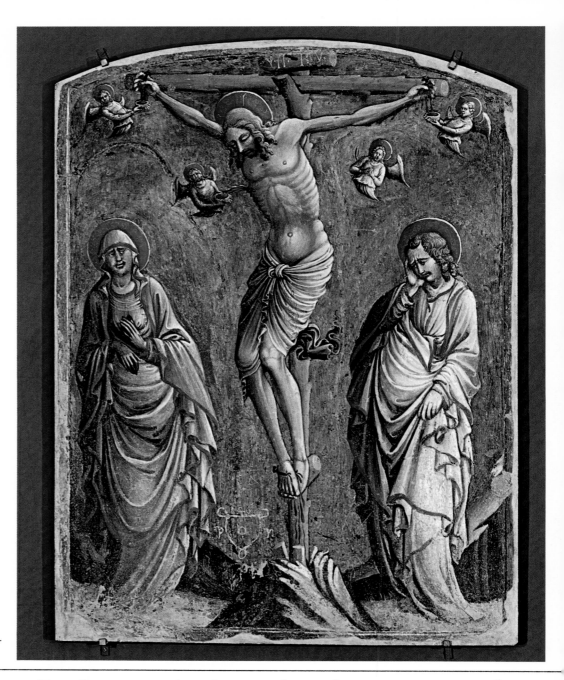

109. Crucifixion. *Fresco and sinopia. Probably by Parri. Italy, Tuscany, 1448.*

But for every crucifixion where the outer pain predominates, there is another where all is swallowed up in divinity and inner peace. At their worst they are chromos, so gaudy and sentimental that Jesus appears in them as neither man nor God but some kind of impossible *tertium quid*. In one of them, for instance, (108) we see him not so much nailed to the cross as posing in front of it like a man in front of a photographer's backdrop. There is something almost sensual about the way the painter has represented his body. The wound of the Roman spear is visible in his side and blood runs down where the nails have been driven, but nothing is allowed to mar the sleek modeling of his pale flesh, the ripe contours of his belly, the way the spotless white cloth has been tied around his loins less to conceal than to exploit their nakedness. The crown of thorns encircles his handsome brow like a silk handkerchief, and his beautifully brushed and glossy hair falls soft over his right breast. A halo glows behind him, and the crude jibe tacked up above him — Jesus of Nazareth, King of the Jews — has become an engraved testimonial.

Something of this same feeling is generated by a fifteenth century fresco (109) where, although there is nothing beautiful about the Jesus who hangs from the slender green cross, there are four little legless angels fluttering in the air about him. They hold chalices in their hands, and the blood they are collecting from his wounds is not for one moment to be mistaken for the blood of a dying man but rather the Blood of the Lamb that will be distributed at the Eucharist.

It is only the rare ones where the divinity and the humanity both shine through, the peace at the heart of the pain, the pain that peace cannot be at peace without enduring. All that is left of one of them is the head and torso (110). The cross has gone. The arms have gone. The wood is pitted and scratched, and most of the paint has long since flaked away. The face is in ruins. Around one cheek and temple there is a dark, scaling discoloration like a bruise. Part of the eyelid is missing. The head has fallen sideways against the stump of a shoulder.

Time has done its worst, and the result is timeless. Our age is full of people for whom the language of religious faith is a dead language and its symbols empty, for whom

FOLLOWING PAGES

110. Corpus Christi. *Walnut wood with traces of polychrome. France, 14th-15th century.*

111. The Crucified. *Woven Straw. Mexican, contemporary.*

112. The Crucifixion. *Felt-tip marker on paper. Nina Ripper, age 7. U.S.A. contemporary.*

the figure of Jesus is vague and remote as a figure in a dream. But for all this it is hard to imagine anyone's looking at this battered relic of the faith of an earlier age without being moved if only by how far from it our age has come. Legless and armless except for those who over the centuries have tried to be his legs and arms, wrecked, powerless except for the power to stir the deepest intuitions and longings of the human heart — if ever there was a man worth dying with and dying for, this is how he should have looked. If ever there should turn out unbe-

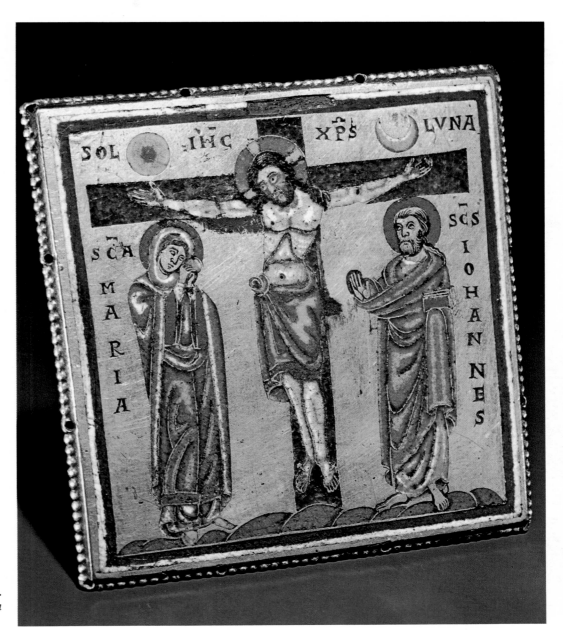

113. Crucifixion with the Virgin and St. John. *Champlevé and cloisonné enamel on copper gilt. Mosan, mid-12th century.*

lievably to be a God of love willing to search for men even in the depths of evil and pain, this is the face we would know him by.

"Thou art the King of Glory, O Christ!" sings out the *Te Deum.* "When thou hadst overcome the sharpness of death, thou didst open the Kingdom of Heaven to all believers," and in woven straw (111) with his halo spiking out like a sunburst and his golden arms thrown high, he rides his cross like a rocket as he shoots toward Heaven.

"When it was evening," Mark writes, "there came a

193

114. The Descent from the Cross. *Tempera and gold leaf on vellum. Germany, Saxony, about 1230.*

115. The Descent from the Cross. *Oakwood, polychromed and gilded. South Netherlands, early 16th century.*

rich man from Aramathea, named Joseph, who also was a disciple of Jesus. He went to Pilate and asked for the body of Jesus. Then Pilate ordered it to be given to him. And Joseph took the body, and wrapped it in a clean linen shroud, and laid it in his own tomb, which he had hewn in the rock; and he rolled a great stone to the door of the tomb, and departed.''

Perhaps it is Joseph who has climbed one of the two shaky ladders and stands there rather precariously with

one shapely calf exposed as he starts to lower Jesus in a

116. The Descent from the Cross. *Bronze appliqué. France, about 1130.*

sling that he holds looped under the chest (115). He has his richly turbaned head turned away as though he doesn't have the heart to look. The body of Jesus is limp in death, and one arm hangs down loose, the pierced hand lower than the knees. On the other ladder, a second man is there to receive the body as Joseph lowers it. Maybe it is Nicodemus, who John says was also present. He is staring at Joseph with an expression of anger as if to say that maybe if he had the stomach to look at what he was doing, he would be doing it better.

117. Mourning over the Dead Christ. *Oakwood, polychromed and gilded. South Netherlands, about 1500.*

In another representation of this next to last station of the cross, a bronze Joseph carries out the grim task alone. He is a short man here, much shorter than Jesus, and though he is braced at the foot of the cross with his feet spread apart to withstand the weight of the body when it falls, you have the feeling that in every sense it will prove too much for him. With its arms spread wide, the body flys above the game little tycoon like a great bird ready to swoop down and carry him off to Paradise.

197   In the most ancient works of Christian art, Jesus is por-

118. Pietà. *Ivory. Probably Spain, 15th century.*

119. Pietà, *detail. Ivory. Probably Spain, 15th century.*

trayed as very young, hardly more than a boy, whereas his mother, as she is represented in the catacombs, for instance, looks like a woman in her forties or fifties. As time went by, however, their positions were reversed with Jesus growing older over the centuries and Mary, younger; until around the thirteenth century, they met briefly as brother and sister, both of them somewhere in their thirties. Maybe it is the fate of every parent to become the child in the end and every child the parent, but that is in any case what happened to them next because by the time this fifteenth

198

century *Pietà* was carved in ivory (118), Jesus had aged considerably. Mary had become a girl, and the son she cradles in her lap is now her father. She wears a shawl over her head. Her young face has passed through grief to the other side. Her expression is composed, almost formally so, and her eyes are closed. It is possible that she has mercifully fallen asleep for a moment. The hand with which she seems to have been holding Jesus to her has relaxed its grip, and his body has slipped forward on her knees with one arm dangling. In another moment she will wake with a start just in time to keep him from falling.

Jesus' neck is arched back awkwardly over his mother's knee so that his head hangs upside down although his hair remains miraculously in place. The wound in his side has exposed three of his ribs. There are the wrinkles of age on his forehead and frown lines between his eyes. Because of the way the end of his nose has chipped off and the way his moustache fans out from the deep cleft on his upper lip, there is something catlike about his face. In his crown of thorns he is King of the Cats, a dead cat tied around the neck of the world to remind it of its guilt for the rest of time, as if it needed reminding. And to remind it of how high its hopes once were and how cruelly they were dashed to the ground. The Messiah lies dead as a doornail across the lap of a sleeping girl. The one who said that he was the light of the world has gone out like a match. The one who they said was the hope of the world is himself now beyond hope.

It was what Mary had feared from the beginning. Even when the Angel of the Annunciation had appeared to her years before, she was greatly troubled by what he told her.

There is reason to suspect that she never fully understood

120. The Dead Christ. *Felt banner. Norman LaLiberté. U.S.A., contemporary.*

what her son was about and would have persuaded him to give it up if she could. Jesus never had much time for her, and when they came to him once to say that his mother was waiting outside, he told them that whoever did the will of his Father in Heaven, that was his mother. Only on the cross did he seem to focus clearly on who she was and on the depths of her need. He told the disciple he loved most to look after her when he was gone and told her that from now on the disciple would be the son to her that he himself had had no time to be what with a world to save,

201

121. Crucifixion and Entombment. *Ivory diptych. France or Flanders, about 1400.*

a death to die. He spoke to her more like her father than like her child, and in losing him she had lost a child and father both. *Pietà* means pity, and the pity of it here in old ivory is that in a moment or two she will wake up, and all the appalling grief of it will come flooding back.

It is almost a relief to her, one imagines, when they lay him in his tomb. In an ivory diptych (121) they have the crucifixion on one panel and the entombment on the other, and the way the diptych is made, you can close it up like a book and fasten it with a clasp. The body of Jesus is laid

202

"The cross
as the crossroads
of
eternity and time."

out for burial, and Mary is reaching down to pull the shroud over his nakedness. She has raised one of his dead hands up to her lips so that she can kiss him goodbye. She is ready now to close once and for all the book of his failed and bewildering life and to let them roll up the great stone to seal it. ☐

122. Christ Carrying the Cross and St. Veronica. *Wood, painted and gilded. Flanders, 15th century.*

FOLLOWING PAGES

123. Head of Christ. *Felt banner. Norman LaLiberté. U.S.A., contemporary.*

124. The Crucified Christ. *Wood, polychromed. U.S.A., 20th century.*

125. Christ Crowned with Thorns. *Bronze cast plaquette. Maurice de Bus. France, about 1955.*

126. Crucifixion. *Wood. Melanesia, contemporary.*

127. Corpus Christi, *detail. Gilt bronze. France, about 1130.*

128. Christ Beneath the Cross, *detail. Embroidered chasuble. Brussels, 16th century.*

129. Pietà. *Bronze. Ivan Mestrović. Yugoslavia, 1962.*

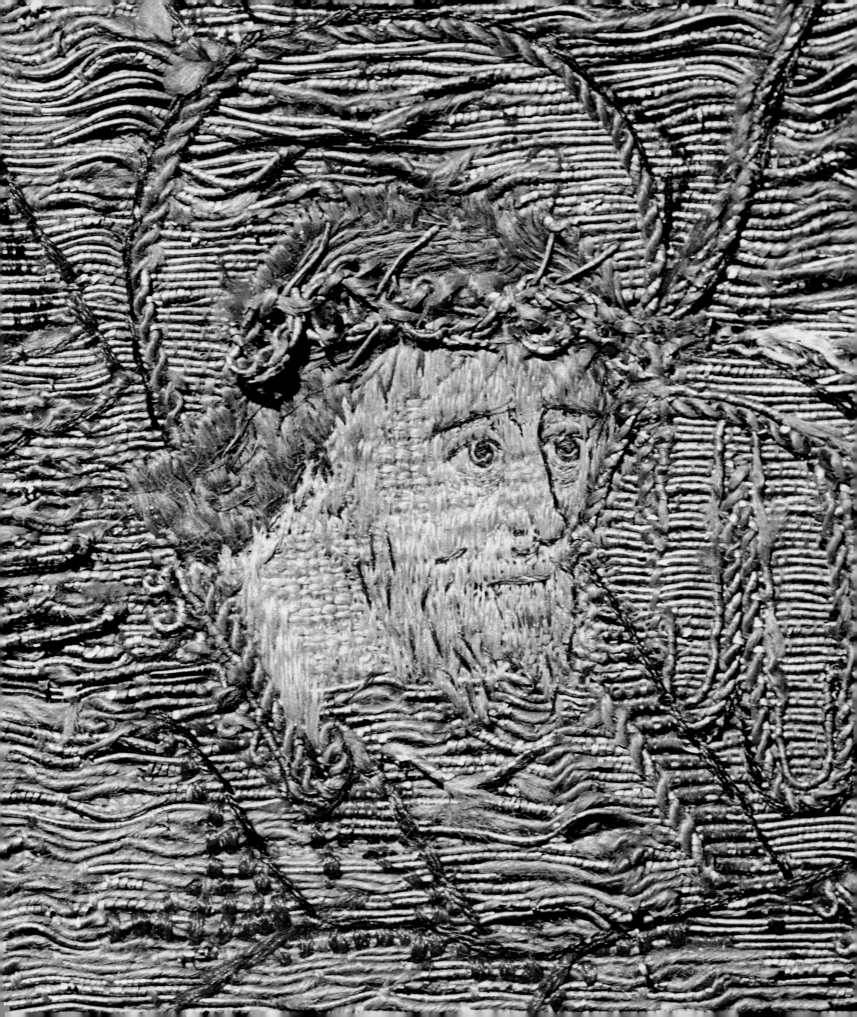

IC XC

ВСЕДЕРЖИТЕЛЬ

ПРИИДЕТЕ БЛГ
СЛОВЕННИ ОЦА
МОЕГО И НАСЛ
СЛЕДУЙТЕ У
ГОТОВАН
ОБ ВАМ

ЦРТВIE
ВСЛОВЕ
НЕ МИРА
ВСАКЪ ВО
СА ИДАСТ
СЛИ ИАСТ

PRECEEDING PAGE

130. Christ Blessing. *Enamel. Russian, style of Byzantine work.*

131. Trinitarian Christ. *Tempera and oil on panel. Flanders, about 1500.*

RESURRECTION

"On the day after Jesus died," Matthew says, "the chief priests and the Pharisees gathered before Pilate and said, 'Sir, we remember how that impostor said, while he was still alive, "After three days I will rise again." Therefore order the sepulchre to be made secure until the third day, lest his disciples go and steal him away, and tell the people, "He has risen from the dead," and the last fraud will be worse than the first.' Pilate said to them, 'You have a guard of soldiers; go, make it as secure as you can.' So they went and made the sepulchre secure by sealing the stone and setting a guard."

When whatever it was that happened that night had happened, the guardsmen came racing back from the tomb to say that it was empty. According to Matthew, the chief priests and the Pharisees bribed them to spread the rumor that the disciples had stolen the corpse under cover of darkness. Pocketing the cash, the soldiers did as they were told, and "this story," Matthew concludes, "has been spread among the Jews to this day."

If this story was a lie, then what was the truth? In the apocryphal Gospel of Peter, which was written a great many years after the event, it is wonderfully told how, far from being asleep, the soldiers were wide awake when all of a sudden the heavens opened and two figures descended in a great cloud of light. The soldiers immediately woke up everybody else who was there sharing the watch with them so that there was a whole crowd of eyewitnesses to vouch for what happened next. The stone at the mouth of the tomb rolled back by itself, and the two glowing figures went in. When they came out again, they were supporting between them a third figure who was followed by a miraculous cross. The heads of the original two "reached into heaven," the account says, "but of him that was led by them . . . it overpassed the heavens."

If Matthew, Mark, Luke and John had wanted to concoct an account appropriate to the occasion, this is very much the kind of account they would probably have concocted, but instead of that they give virtually no account at all. In the canonical gospels no story is told of how the body of Jesus disappeared from the tomb. All that is said is that by the time the women got there, the stone had been rolled back and it was empty. What followed was chaos — dim figures flickering through the dawn, voices calling out, the sound of running feet. When the women got back to Jerusalem and gasped it all out to the disciples, Luke says that the disciples considered their words "an idle tale, and they did not believe them."

Who knows what the truth of it was? Maybe somebody really did steal the body at night while the guards were asleep, and Matthew is only attempting to explain it away. Maybe the apocryphal Gospel of Peter with its angels and miracles is closer to the facts than in our sophistication we are capable of imagining. Maybe it is the New Testament account with its picture of confusion and disbelief that rings most authentically — nobody ever knew exactly

what happened because nobody was there to see it. Or

132. Icon. Oil on wood with gold over-frame. Russian, 18th century.

maybe the tomb was empty because Jesus had never been put there in the first place but was just thrown into a common ditch with the two thieves who were crucified with him.

The earliest reference to the resurrection is Saint Paul's, and he makes no mention of an empty tomb at all. But the fact of the matter is that in a way it hardly matters how the body of Jesus came to be missing because in the last analysis what convinced the people that he had risen from the dead was not the absence of his corpse but his living

219

presence. And so it has been ever since.

Luke tells how, on that same third day, two of the disciples were on their way to a town called Emmaus a few miles out of Jerusalem when they were joined by a man they did not recognize. While they walked, he talked with them about the whole sad story of the Messiah and how he had died. When evening came and they reached their destination, the stranger indicated that he was going to keep on a while longer, but they persuaded him to stop and have supper with them. It was only when he blessed the bread and then broke it and gave it to them that they saw who he was.

The table was laid with a turquoise cloth (133), and a big yellow fish had been brought in on a platter with its goggle eyes glazed in death. As soon as Jesus took the loaf of bread in his hands, one of the disciples lept up from his chair and grabbed hold of the table to steady himself. The other remained sitting in a kind of trance. They could hardly see the face of the stranger for the great sunflower of light that suddenly blossomed out behind it, but they saw enough to know that it was not a stranger who was standing there. The moment they knew who it was, he was gone.

On another occasion Thomas saw him too, of all the disciples the one who manages somehow to put his thumb on our hearts, the one from Missouri. He was known as the Twin, John says, and in some sense he is the twin of us all, this doubting Thomas. The disciples were hiding out in Jerusalem somewhere, scared out of their wits that the authorities who had taken care of Jesus would be arriving any moment to take care of them. They had bolted the door and were listening for the dreaded sound of footsteps

133. Supper at Emmaus. *Oil on canvas.*
Ivo Dulčič. Yugoslavia, 1916.

on the stair when suddenly Jesus was among them. He stood there in their midst — always *in the midst*, this man, turning up when they least expected him, maybe least wanted him — and told them to breathe in his breath, his holy breath and spirit, so that they could go out into the world again and perform his holy work. They all heard what he said with their ears and saw how he looked with their eyes except Thomas, who was not there at the time, maybe because it was like him always to be somewhere 221 else at the crucial moment. When he came back a while

134. Doubting Thomas. *Walrus Ivory. Germany, Cologne, about 1130-1140.*

later, they told him what had happened. Thomas said, "Unless I see in his hands the print of the nails, and place my finger in the mark of the nails, and place my hand in his side, I will not believe." Thomas, our twin.

A week or so later Jesus appeared to them again, and this time Thomas was there. Several of the disciples seem to have been reading at the time because they still have their books in their hands as they stand up to greet their risen leader. But Thomas does not seem to have been read-

222 ing. Maybe he was staring out the window at the crene-

lated city wall which looked at that distance like a child's toy with its little medieval turrets and gatehouses of walrus ivory (134).

Jesus says, "Put your finger here, and see my hands; and put out your hand and place it in my side." To make it easier for Thomas, he undoes the top of his robe and holds his right arm up so that it will be out of the way. Thomas crouches down to touch the wounded place, and as he touches it, and only then, he says, "My Lord and my God!" and Jesus says, "Have you believed because you have seen me? Blessed are those who have not seen and yet believe."

It is the story of our lives, of course, as in some queer way the whole Bible is the story of our lives. Which of us hasn't known the innocence of Eden and tasted the sweetness of the forbidden tree? Which of us hasn't heard the angry thundering of the prophets in our own souls and like Israel hoped against hope for a savior to deliver us from, if nothing else, ourselves? But Thomas's story is especially our story. Unless we see with our own eyes, we will not believe because we cannot believe, cannot believe fully anyway, cannot believe in a sense that affects the way we live our lives. Nearly two thousand Easters have taken place since Thomas's day, two thousand years' worth of people proclaiming that the tomb was empty and the dead Christ alive among men to heal, to sustain, to transform. But it is not enough. If men are to believe in his resurrection in a way that really matters, they must somehow see him for themselves. And wherever men have so believed in his resurrection, it is because in some sense they have so seen him. Now as then, it is not his absence from the empty tomb that convinces men but the shadow at least of his presence in their empty lives.

223

135. Christ Blessing. *Limestone. U.S.A., 20th century.*

In another apocryphal gospel, this one ascribed to Doubting Thomas himself, Jesus is depicted as saying, "Cleave a piece of wood, and I am there. Lift up the stone, and you will find me there." In other words, there is no place on earth too outlandish to find him in, no place on earth but where, in their outlandish yearning to see and thus believe, men have not believed that they have seen him. Blessed are they who have not seen as Thomas saw, and yet with the eyes of their yearning and their faith have seen enough.

224

136. Christ over New York City. *Paint on slatted steel door. Ukrainian-American, 20th century.*

In a parking lot, for instance: through the weeping of a willow, yellow with spring. He is hedged round with dead leaves, a row of broken stones. There are five cars parked near him, but they are all empty, their windows blank as stares. There he stands as white as light with his hands stretched out in front of him as though he is feeling his way in the dark or back into time again (135).

Or on the slatted overhead door of some garage or warehouse made to roll up out of the way so that much of the time he lies flat on his back out of sight (136). But here he

137. Christ the Judge. *Stone. Trent, Cathedral Church, about 1400.*

has been rolled down at full length and is represented as an enormous figure wading up to his chest in the dark sky, brooding over the skyline of a city. The style is Early Billboard, and Jesus has been costumed and wigged for the leading role in a Cecil B. DeMille epic, but you cannot go in or out without one way or another coming to terms with him and with the inscription blocked out in Greek and English above his head: BEHOLD, JESUS COME QUICKLY. Of all the thousands upon thousands of words in the Bible, these are the last words. Thus the whole vast

226

138. The Face of Jesus. *Plaster plate. Norman LaLiberté. U.S.A., contemporary.*

compendium of poetry and history, legend and law, ends with a cry for help.

Lift up the stone and you will find him there carved into the stone façade of some medieval church. Crumbling and pigeon-spattered, he crouches in judgment with one hand raised in admonition and the other holding the Book of Life (137). Centuries of weather have broken his nose and split his lip, but they have not softened the wild intensity of his stone eyes which start out of their sockets as he stares down at history.

139. Christ of the Apocalypse, *detail. Embroidered altarcloth. Germany, Altenburg-an-der-Lahn, about 1350.*

From the surface of a ceramic plate (138) he stares up like the Man in the Moon. His face is so carelessly scored into the clay that it could almost be only by accident a design, only to the suggestible a face at all, let alone the face of Jesus. "Have you believed because you have seen me?" he asked Thomas, and then "Blessed are those who have not seen . . ." except ambiguously, obscurely, never sure whether what they have seen is the holiness at the heart of reality itself or only a shadow cast by their longing for holiness at the heart. John says that when Mary

228

Magdalen saw him at the tomb that early dawn, she thought at first that he was the gardener. Maybe for the rest of her life she was never entirely sure.

The likeness embroidered into a six hundred-year-old altar cloth (139) has been laundered and pressed almost beyond recognition. It is Jesus in his glory, the Christ of the Apocalypse whom no language is too marvelous to describe, no images too preposterous and resplendent to embody. "Like a son of man," the Book of Revelation says of him, and then a breathless cataract of words: "clothed with a long robe and with a golden girdle round his breast; his head and his hair were white as snow; his eyes were like a flame of fire, his feet were like burnished bronze, refined as in a furnace, and his voice was like the sound of many waters; in his right hand he held seven stars, from his mouth issued a sharp two-edged sword, and his face was like the sun shining in full strength."

His face here has faded to the color of moonlight, and there is a crease down the center of it where the cloth has been folded year after year. The seven stars have long since slipped out of his right hand and are barely visible against the pale sky behind him. The two-edged sword issuing from his mouth has fallen apart into two swords with which, at his coming again to judge both the quick and the dead, he will slay the wicked. The linen is threadbare, and in one corner you can see a darn the shape of a wreath where it has been mended. Blessed are those whose vision is threadbare at best.

A pair of angels fly behind him with two of the instruments of his passion — the cross and the spear — as Jesus sits in the judgment seat (140). Below him there are more

angels trumpeting the dead from their graves while nearby

140. The Coronation of the Virgin and the Last Judgment. *Ivory diptych. France, probably Paris, about 1275.*

141. The Death of the Virgin, *detail. Oil on wood with gold overframe. Russian, 18th century.*

Satan looks on as already the souls of the damned are being thrust bare-bottomed into the gaping maw of Hell. Fresh from her coronation as Queen of Heaven, the Virgin Mary is on her knees offering prayers of intercession for them, and her son has thrown up his hands in gentle dismay. When Mary died, Jesus came in person to take her soul in his arms and carry her with him to Paradise, perhaps to make it up to her for all the years of his neglect. On a painted wooden panel heavily overlaid with gold we see them with their roles completely reversed at last — he

231

mothering her in his arms and she a babe in swaddling clothes (141).

In one of the most powerful passages in the Gospels, Jesus while still on earth foretells this scene of the Last Judgment. All the nations of the earth are drawn up before the Son of Man, he says, and the Son of Man will separate them from one another as a shepherd separates the sheep from the goats. It is the principle by which he separates them that split history in two. Placing the souls of the righteous on his right hand, he says to them, "I was hungry and you gave me food, I was thirsty and you gave me drink, I was a stranger and you welcomed me, I was naked and you clothed me, I was sick and you visited me, I was in prison and you came to me," and when the righteous turn to him and ask when they can ever have had the opportunity to do such things for him, he answers them by saying, "As you did it to one of the least of these my brethren, you did it to me." And then the unrighteous, of course. "I was hungry and you gave me no food," he says — thirsty, a stranger, naked and sick and in prison — and to their shuddering question *Lord, when?* he has a shuddering answer: "As you did it not to one of the least of these, you did it not to me."

Thus for Jesus the only distinction between men that ultimately matters seems to be not whether they are churchgoers or non-churchgoers, communists or capitalists, Catholics or Protestants or Jews, but do they or do they not love — love not in the sense of an emotion so much as in the sense of an act of the will, the loving act of willing another's good even, if need arise, at the expense of their own. "Hell is the suffering of being unable to

love," said old Father Zossima or, as John puts it in his first

142. The Sacred Heart. *Rug. U.S.A., 20th century*.

epistle, "He who does not love remains in death." It is no wonder that enthroned in the ivory diptych with his mother on her knees at his side, Jesus throws up his hands in dismay.

As you did it to one of the least of these my brethren, you did it to me. Just as Jesus appeared at his birth as a helpless child that the world was free to care for or destroy, so now he appears in his resurrection as the pauper, the prisoner, the stranger: appears in every form of human need that the world is free to serve or to ignore.

The risen Christ is Christ risen in his glory and enthroned in all this glorious canvas, stained glass, mosaic as Redeemer and Judge. But he is also Christ risen in the shabby hearts of those who, although they have never touched the mark of the nails, have been themselves so touched by him that they believe anyway. However faded and threadbare, what they have seen of him is at least enough to get their bearings by.

Against a crimson bubble bath of clouds where picture postcard *putti* play, a brilliantined Jesus with soulful eyes points at his chest where his Sacred Heart hangs like a giant strawberry crowned with cross and flames and encircled with thorns. There is nothing faded and threadbare here, but in its lurid and touching tastelessness it speaks much the same word about those who have seen enough to know at least that the heart is sacred because he has touched it (142).

Many would settle for this. Many would settle for the Resurrection as a metaphor for the unconquerable power of love in the world, for the undying spirit of Jesus which still has the power to touch and guide the hearts of men as the spirit of Lincoln does, or Joan of Arc, or Martin Luther King. Jesus triumphs as virtue triumphs, is alive as hope is alive, keeps returning to the world as springtime returns. Many a Christian sermon has been preached along such lines, and there are many outside the faith as well as inside it who would be willing to say amen. But not Paul.

It is no wonder that so many people deplore him as the one who defiled the pure stream of Jesus' teachings with unnecessary theological obscurities. It is no wonder that so many recoil from his arrogance, his ill temper, his views on women, the divisive polemics that he fired off like buck-

143. Head of Christ. *Tempera and oil on panel. Reverse of the Pala d'Oro, San Marco. Venetian artist, 14th century.*

144. Christ in a Mandorla. *Stained glass. England, 12th century.*

shot in those marvelous, punch-drunk letters with which he peppered the missionary churches of his time. But for better or worse, Paul spoke out what he believed to be the truth regardless of consequences, and for better or worse the truth as he spoke it has remained all these years the classic expression of Christian orthodoxy.

About the Resurrection Paul could hardly have made himself clearer. "If Christ has not been raised, then our preaching is in vain and your faith is in vain," he wrote to the Corinthians. "If for this life only we have hope in

Christ, we are of all men most to be pitied. But in fact Christ has been raised from the dead, the first fruits of those who have fallen asleep. For as by man came death, by a man has come also the resurrection of the dead. For as in Adam all die, so also in Christ shall all be made alive."

For Paul the Resurrection was no metaphor; it was the power of God. And when he spoke of Jesus as raised from the dead, he meant Jesus alive and at large in the world not as some shimmering ideal of human goodness or the achieving power of hopeful thought but as the very power of life itself. If the life that was in Jesus died on the cross; if the love that was in him came to an end when his heart stopped beating; if the truth that he spoke was no more if no less timeless than the great truths of any time; if all that he had in him to give to the world was a little glimmer of light to make bearable the inexorable approach of endless night — then all was despair.

To make sure that nobody missed the point, Paul spelled it out still further in his shattering bluntness. In speaking of the Resurrection of Christ as supremely real, it was supremely of Christ that he was speaking and of Christ's glory, but it was also of man and man's glory. If Jesus had been raised from the dead, then all who had something of his life in them would be raised from the dead with him. If on the other hand death was the end for Jesus, it would be the end for all men whether they had his life in them or not; and if that was the case, then in the long run what did Jesus matter, what did anything matter? Paul makes the alternatives as sharp and simple as that and leaves no doubt which one he believes. "Lo, I tell you a mystery," he writes. "We shall all be changed in a moment, in the

237 twinkling of an eye, at the last trumpet . . . for this perish-

145. Christ Enthroned. *Gold coin. Byzantium.*

146. Christ Enthroned with Saints and a Donor. *Ivory. Germany or North Italy, probably by 968.*

able nature must put on the imperishable, and this mortal nature must put on immortality . . . Thanks be to God, who gives us the victory through our Lord Jesus Christ."

Gives *us* the victory, he says, so the last picture of the risen Christ should be the one that has us in it. We are in it in the form of the donor, the one who got into the picture because he was the one who donated it (146). Jesus is seated on the curve of the earth with his saints about him, and the donor is approaching from the wings. He is a

238 rather funny looking little man wearing his best hat, and

he is well aware that if the truth were known, he has no right in the world to be there. He is so overawed by his surroundings that his legs have given out on him and one of the saints has had to come up from behind and take him by the elbow to keep him from falling flat. He is afraid he may make a terrible fool of himself, but at the same time there is an expression of great dignity in his face. It is the dignity of a small man who knows that he has no place among the great but who is there anyway and determined to make the best of it. It is not a dignity that is his by nature but a dignity that has been conferred upon him. It is Jesus who is conferring it as he reaches down to take him by the hand. One is struck by a curious resemblance between them.

The face of Jesus is a face that belongs to us the way our past belongs to us. It is a face that we belong to if only as to the one face out of the past that has perhaps had more to do with the shaping of our present than any other. According to Paul, the face of Jesus is our own face finally, the face we will all come to look like a little when the kingdom comes and we are truly ourselves at last, truly the brothers and sisters of one another and the children of God.

All those faces — they come drifting back at us like dreams: the solemn child in his mother's arms, the young man scattering words and miracles like seed, the old man eating for the last time with his old friends, the Jew retching out his life from the cross of his shame.

What words do we face him with? Maybe the best are the words the Bible ends with: *Come Lord Jesus.* The unbeliever can say them along with the believer. Why not? If he exists somewhere beyond men's ancient longing for him and has wings to come on, let him come then, with healing in his wings. Or maybe the best is not words at all but all these images that are the wordless, eloquent, tongue-tied, clumsy, joyous and grieving cry of centuries.

And what will be his last words here to us? Let them be a little crazy because in terms of the world's grim sanity, he is a little crazy indeed, and all who follow him are too. Let them be the words to the hymn that according to the apocryphal Acts of John he sang to his disciples at their last meal:

Glory be to thee, Father.
Glory be to thee, Word. Glory be to thee, Grace. Amen.
Glory be to thy glory. Amen.

I would be saved, and I would save. Amen.
I would be loosed, and I would loose. Amen.
I would be wounded, and I would wound. Amen.
I would be born, and I would bear. Amen.
I would eat, and I would be eaten. Amen.
I would hear, and I would be heard. Amen.
Grace danceth. I would pipe. Dance ye all. Amen.
I would mourn. Lament ye all. Amen.
Whoso danceth not, knoweth not what cometh to pass. Amen.
I would flee, and I would stay. Amen.
I would adorn, and I would be adorned. Amen.
I would be united, and I would unite. Amen.
A house I have not, and I have houses. Amen.
A lamp am I to thee that beholdest me. Amen.
A mirror am I to thee that perceivest me. Amen.
A door am I to thee that knockest at me. Amen.
A way am I to thee a wayfarer. Amen.

THUS, MY BELOVED, HAVING DANCED WITH US, THE LORD WENT FORTH.

``*Thus, my beloved, having danced with us, the Lord went forth.*''

147. Christ the Judge. *Bronze. Church doors of San Zeno, Verona, early 12th century.*

FOLLOWING PAGES

148. "Volto di Cristo". *Bronze. Primo Conti. Italy, contemporary.*

149. *The Master of the Fogg Pietà. Fresco, sinopia drawing. Florence, mid-15th century.*

150. Image of Christ. *Wood. Austria, 18th century.*

151. Christ with the Monogram. *Mosaic pavement. England, Hinton St. Mary (Dorset), probably 6th-7th century.*

152. Christ Enthroned. *Cloisonné enamel and gold. Russian, in the style of 12th century works.*

153. Head of Christ. *Bronze, enamel, and mosaic. Bufano. USA, 20th century.*

154. "Volto di Cristo". *Mosaic. Gino Severini. Italy, 20th century.*

"These images are the wordless, eloquent, tongue-tied, clumsy, joyous and grieving cry of centuries."

ACKNOWLEDGMENTS

We are especially grateful to the Metropolitan Museum of Art *and the* Vatican Museum of Contemporary Christian Art *for their invaluable assistance.*

We are indebted to many people who assisted in the completion of this book. They include: Oliver Allen; Dr. and Mrs. Franz Erlach; Mr. and Mrs. James Cronin; J. H. Plumb; Kenneth Clark; E. H. Gombrich; W. H. Auden; Carmen Gomez-Moreno; Charles Little; Robert Morton; Marjorie Weeks; Terence Cardinal Cooke; Margaret Stafford; Monsignor Eugene Clark; Luigino Brocato; Judith Lapiner; Elizabeth Ames Nelson; Julianne Splain; Maurice Lavanoux; Sister Marcella and Sister Louise Trevison of Maryknoll; Robert Northshield; Sister Maria Rabalais; Jeanne Heiberg; Dr. George Price; John Chancellor; Father Edward O'Brien.

254

PICTURE CREDITS

All photography is by Lee Boltin except where indicated.

2. Metropolitan Museum of Art (New York) Cited hereafter as: MMA

3. MMA

4. Vatican Museum of Contemporary Christian Art Cited hereafter as: VMCCA

5. Coll. Cronin

6. Notre-Dame-des-Fontaines, La Brigue, France (Photo: Pierre Boulat)

7. Pulpit, Cathedral, Siena

8. MMA, Bequest of Mrs. Edward S. Stillman Harkness, 1950

9. MMA, The Cloisters Collection, Purchase 1954 (Photo: MMA)

10. Oratory of San Galgano, Montesiepi

11. Church of San Lorenzo, Arezzo

12. Treasury, Cathedral of Tournai

13. MMA, Gift of J. Pierpont Morgan, 1917 (Photo: MMA)

14. Coll. Cronin

15. MMA, The Michael Friedsam Collection, 1931 (Photo: MMA)

16. MMA (Photo: MMA)

17. Private Collection

18. VMCCA

19. Rockefeller Chapel, University of Chicago

20. Church of Santissimi Apostoli, Florence

21. Private Collection

22. Treasury, Cathedral of Tournai

23. MMA

24. Coll. Maurice Lavanoux

25. MMA, Gift of J. Pierpont Morgan, 1917

26. Maryknoll Sisters' Museum, Maryknoll, New York

27. Coll. Maurice Lavanoux

28. Present whereabouts unknown

29. Maryknoll Sisters' Museum, Maryknoll, New York

30. Coll. Maurice Lavanoux

31. Private Collection

32. MMA, Gift of J. Pierpont Morgan, 1917

33. Ethnological Museum, Vatican City

34. Ethnological Museum, Vatican City

35. MMA

36. VMCCA

37. Coll. Erlach

38. VMCCA

39. VMCCA

40. VMCCA

41. Private Collection

42. Coll. Maurice Lavanoux

43. Coll. Erlach

44. Coll. Cronin

45. Coll. Maurice Lavanoux

46. Coll. Maurice Lavanoux

47. Coll. Cronin

48. Coll. Lavanoux

49. Cavendish Square, London

50. MMA, The Cloisters

51. Church of Notre-Dame, Huy (Belgium)

52. National Gallery of Art, Washington, D.C. (Photo: National Gallery)

53. Private Collection

54. MMA (Photo: MMA)

55. Private Collection

56. MMA, Gift of William H. Webb, 1885 (Photo: MMA)

57. MMA

58. Cathedral Baptistery, Florence

59. Ethnological Museum, Vatican City

60. Archepiscopal Museum, Ravenna

61. Coll. Cronin

62. Trollhättan, Sweden (Photo: Nationalmuseum)

63. MMA

64. Nationalmuseum, Sweden (Photo: Nationalmuseum)

65. Private Collection

66. MMA, Gift of William H. Webb, 1885 (Photo: MMA)

67. VMCCA

68. H. Shickman Gallery, New York

69. MMA (Photo: MMA)

70. Notre-Dame-des-Fontaines, La Brigue, France (Photo: Pierre Boulat)

71. National Gallery, Washington, D.C., The Samuel H. Kress Collection (Photo: National Gallery)

72. MMA

73. MMA

74. MMA

75. Nationalmuseum, Sweden (Photo: Nationalmuseum)

76. Private Collection

77. VMCCA

78. Ethnological Museum, Vatican City

79. VMCCA

80. Ethnological Museum, Vatican City

81. MMA

82. MMA

83. MMA (Photo: MMA)

84. Coll. Clain-Stefanelli

85. National Gallery, Washington, D.C. (Photo: National Gallery)

86. Notre-Dame-des-Fontaines, La Brigue, France (Photo: Pierre Boulat)

87. MMA

88. Ethnological Museum, Vatican City

89. VMCCA

90. Coll. Erlach

91. Church of San Zeno, Verona, Italy

92. Coll. Erlach

93. Rockefeller Chapel, University of Chicago

94. Nationalmuseum, Sweden (Photo: Nationalmuseum)

95. MMA

96. VMCCA

97. Coll. Cronin

98. Notre-Dame-des-Fontaines, La Brigue, France (Photo: Pierre Boulat)

99. VMCCA

100. MMA

101. Ethnological Museum, Vatican City

102. Private Collection Antwerp

103. VMCCA

104. Whaling Museum, Nantucket, Massachusetts

105. MMA

106. MMA, Gift of J. Pierpont Morgan, 1917

107. VMCCA

108. Museo del Prado, Madrid

109. Palazzo Communale, Arezzo

110. MMA

111. Coll. Cronin

112. Private Collection

113. MMA

114. MMA

115. MMA

116. MMA

117. MMA

118. MMA

119. MMA

120. Rockefeller Chapel, University of Chicago

121. MMA

122. MMA

123. Rockefeller Chapel, University of Chicago

124. Graymoor Retreat, Garrison, New York

125. Coll. Clain-Stefanelli

126. Ethnological Museum, Vatican City

127. MMA

128. Coll. Erlach

129. VMCCA

130. MMA

131. H. Shickman Gallery, New York

132. Formerly A la Vieille Russie, New York

133. VMCCA

134. MMA

135. Graymoor Retreat, Garrison, New York

136. New York City storefront

137. Private Collection

138. Coll. Cronin

139. MMA

140. MMA

141. Maryknoll Sisters' Museum, Maryknoll, New York

142. Colorado, Gift Shop

143. Church of San Marco, Venice

144. All Souls' College, Oxford

145. Smithsonian Institution, Washington, D.C.

146. MMA

147. Church of San Zeno, Verona

148. VMCCA

149. Church of Sant'Ambrogio, Florence

150. Coll. Erlach

151. British Museum

152. MMA

153. San Francisco

154. VMCCA